D1376530

Creative Themes

Young Children Learning

Creative Themes

A Book of Ideas for Teachers

by Henry Pluckrose

 Evans Brothers Limited, London

TO RITA
AND HILARY
AND THE CHILDREN THEY TEACH

Printed in Great Britain by G. A. Pindar & Son Ltd., Scarborough
237 28647 5

PR 1809

Contents

55431

Acknowledgements

I should like to record my thanks to the following people for their help in the preparation of this book: Hilary Devonshire for supplying a number of the examples of childrens' writing included in the text; J. Parry Harvey for permission to include photographs which originally appeared in Teacher's World; G. W. Hales for his excellent photographs; F. Peacock and R. Tingle for their help and advice in the compilation of the suggestion lists for the prose and poetry sections and Cicely Tipple for the care she has taken in the preparation of the typescript.

The Frontispiece is reproduced by kind permission of the International Wool Secretariat. The photographs at the beginning of each section are reproduced by kind permission of the following: Will Green, J. Allan Cash, Paul Popper Ltd., the British Museum and the British Interplanetary Society.

By the Same Author

Oil Pastel Techniques	Dryad Press
Creative Arts and Crafts	Macdonald
Let's Make Pictures	Mills and Boon
Let's Work Large	Mills and Boon
Introducing Acrylic Painting	Batsford
Introducing Crayon Techniques	Batsford
with F. Peacock . . .	
Projects Through Craft (Books 1 – 4)	Macdonald

Illustrations

Introduction

'When involved in a creative act one feels his own strength and power as a human being; one feels his own uniqueness in relation to his environment. How different this is from those moments when you await the order or instructions of others; when you stand helplessly by while the machine goes through its operations doing something over which you have little or no control.'

Jerome Hausman

'Education in the melting pot . . .' a newspaper headline typical of our time. We are poised to make a great leap forward – in nursery education, perhaps, or special provision for deprived areas, by completely restructuring education for the adolescent . . . or teacher training or . . . . the list of possibilities has no limit. Here manpower and economic resources are earmarked so that our young people can be helped realise their innate potential to develop fully into mature, balanced, creative human beings. And yet what a contradiction all this seems to be when we think of our world as it is today. Vast sums are spent on attempts to conquer space and reach the moon – while millions here on earth live on the verge of starvation having little chance to develop physically, let alone intellectually. In the name of Peace and Freedom our scientists prepare quicker, cheaper and more efficient means of destroying the very life we teachers and parents are striving to foster.

Indeed even on a more insular note this divergence of purpose is apparent. On the one hand we embrace a philosophy of individual freedom within a framework of social conscience and mutual responsibility. We pay lip service to the uniqueness of the individual, to the importance of the creative processes which give life its purpose and prevent us from becoming little more than automatons in a computer-dominated world. All the time, however, the mores of society seem to demand little more than housing, education, entertainment, newspapers and magazines – for the masses. Comfortable sameness is much more acceptable – being easier to live with and to cater for – than the spirit of individuality (which surely is to be found in all men of character whether they be genius or no).

Over the past eight years I suppose I may claim that I have to some extent been able to opt out of the conventional teaching situation and try (albeit at a very rudimentary level) to provide children with an environment in which their instinct for making things and expressing themselves has been allowed to flower. In a nineteenth century school building in a poor district of South London I worked for a Headteacher, Frank Peacock, who gave me the opportunity to experiment in an atmosphere of calm appraisal and professional security. Here I learnt what could be done to stimulate the imagination of childhood and how through a curriculum rich in painting, free dance, drama, poetry, prose, music and model-making children could be helped to discover their individuality, their particular skills, their gifts.

After six years I moved from this school, built to implement the provisions of Forster's Education Act, to one created for the rich summer of Primary Education in post-Plowden Britain. No doors, few barriers between age groups, display bays and purpose-built furniture – a school built to meet the needs of children as the previous one had been to meet the needs of teachers.

It is from the amalgam of these two contrasting personal experiences that I have written the first part of this book of themes. The ideas are not meant to be slavishly followed. They have been prepared with the aim of giving teachers starting points from which creative work can develop. My experience – if it be of any worth – is that it is not buildings which matter, though a sink in the room helps and a display board is better than a glass partition for doing justice to children's pictures. Rather should we concentrate upon the learning situations which arise within the group and the relationships which are established between teacher and taught. It is these emotive things which cannot be built for and are virtually impossible to assess that are the very threads from which a creative environment is woven.

It would be illogical of me not to welcome new buildings and the provision of a richer environment for young people (being headteacher of an exciting new school surely suggests I have no axe to grind here). But I do wish to make most strongly the point that it is the approach to teaching content and method which needs our particular consideration. I hope that the avenues suggested in this collection of themes will be of some use to teachers in new schools and in old, for the traditionalist and the avant-garde.

Finally as a teacher employed by the Inner London Education Authority I must state that the Authority is in no way responsible for the ideas expressed above or in the chapters which follow.

H.P.

Creative Themes

Approaches

'To the small child everything exists to be explored, experimented with, tested, assessed, remembered and thereby learnt.'

Sybil Marshall

'It's all very well to show us pictures your children have painted and to explain the techniques employed,' said a teacher at a discussion group I was chairing, 'but one cannot produce really exciting work in a vacuum. How do you provide in the confines of a classroom an environment in which creative work in all its aspects will flourish?'

Although I remember feeling that my answer was most inadequate I hope I made my questioner realise that I was very sympathetic towards the problem she posed. Creativity is a topic which has been receiving a great deal of attention on both sides of the Atlantic. David Holbrook, Sybil Marshall and Herbert Read in England and Torrence, Lowenfield, Guilford, Getzels and Jackson in America, have devoted much time to analysing its many different aspects.

But whatever prompts our interest in the subject I believe that we must begin by examining the needs, interests and abilities of the children we teach. This might appear too obvious to need stating but in my experience child development is not as widely studied in our colleges of education as it might be (on the grounds, I understand, that this should be a topic studied 'in depth' on in-service courses taken some time after the student has qualified 'when he will appreciate the subject more fully'). When preparing talks on creative work I am often surprised by the topicality of much of the report on the Consultative Committee of the Primary School (1928-1931) – 'The Primary School should not be regarded merely as a preparatory department for the subsequent stage and the courses should be planned and conditioned – not mainly by the supposed requirements of the secondary stage nor by the exigencies of the examination at eleven but by the needs of the child at that particular phase in his physical and mental development.'

To me this suggests that one of the prime requirements of the Primary School teacher is to be able to appreciate the innate qualities and characteristics of the children in his class for I believe that creative work can only come where the teaching situation takes the child's needs, aptitudes and interests fully into account, i.e. we should begin with the child and build the curriculum round him rather than take a curriculum and fit the child to it.

What are these characteristics? One of the most prosaic descriptions of the primary school child is contained in the above-mentioned report – 'a little workman looking for jobs to do'. He has also been described as an embryo scientist, an explorer and an investigator with a great desire to touch and to see, to experience and to understand . . . a sort of human elephant-child full of insatiable curiosity. This naturally enquiring mind is backed by vast quantities of energy, a love of words both written and spoken and a vivid imagination for which art, model making, writing and drama provide a natural outlet. These qualities, which can be seen most clearly in the young child when he is playing, provide a natural framework for learning and if we can harness them fully the child will be so deeply involved that his creative powers will flower. (An excellent essay on play with a purpose was written by Phyllis Hostler and is contained in *The World of Children*, an anthology published by Paul Hamlyn.)

It is impossible to plan any programme of learning unless we take fully into account 'the needs of the child at that particular phase in his physical and mental development'. Thus our first task is to look critically at our own classrooms. Within the physical limitations of the building are we providing an environment which will allow the child's interests to develop to the full? Pictures, exhibitions and displays of books, children's models and collections can be used to brighten even the oldest classroom. Old buildings often offer as much as their modern counterparts in this respect; at least they allow for improvisation which is invariably the starting point for lively learning.

The teacher will also need to see that a wide range of materials is available. Such things as paint, paper and brushes, clay, plasticine, wood, wire and cane will need to be supplemented with junk materials as varied as packing boxes, straws, wool and cotton reels. Tools for shaping and cutting will also be required as well as reliable adhesives and pastes. This is a very basic list – which could be extended almost endlessly. The teacher should try to make himself aware of a great range of materials so that he can make them available to individual children when the need arises. This may mean regular visits to educational exhibitions to see just what things are in the catalogues (for example the new acrylic colours and adhesives add a new dimension to children's picture making and modelling); attending courses and (if the teacher be that sort of person) experimenting for himself with such things as wax crayons, chalk, powder colour and soap. Before leaving this aspect of environment we should dismiss for ever the idea that there are some things which are best left for the secondary school. If the child is gifted at drawing by all means supply scraper board or cartridge paper and a range of good quality pencils; if painting is his forte is it unrealistic to allow him to experiment in oils? (After all we don't stop a child reading Charles Dickens or the poetry of D. H. Lawrence simply because he is not yet twelve.)

If we provide sufficient stimulation – both visual and practical – we do not need to be artists or craftsmen ourselves to get children to create. Our aim should be to make the classroom, to quote Pestalozzi, a workshop – a place which is interesting, provocative, child-centred[1]. Our task is to see that each child works at a level suitable to his particular stage of development,

[1] We have still not reached the ideal situation outlined in Ministry of Education pamphlet No. 6, 1946, *Art Education*. 'The classrooms should be places of real activity and the general purpose rooms should have all the fitments needed – water, gas, storage for tools and equipment, for exhibiting work, furniture which can be easily moved and stacked away.'

2

at the same time observing carefully the interests peculiar to individual children. Does John like working with wire, scraps and junk or does he prefer the formality of cane or leather-craft? Does Mary like working large with a big brush on expanses of sugar paper or with water colour and squirrel brushes? It is a source of never-ending wonder what materials quite young children will handle successfully. I have seen eight-year-olds confidently controlling an electric kiln, nine-year-olds using graver on wood blocks and ten-year-olds adapting simple dry-point techniques with a flair which would astonish the established craftsman.

Thus even within the narrow confines of the graphic arts – as contained in the examples above – children come near to a realisation of their innate creative potential. But creativity embraces far more than wire and clay, paint and plaster. It should flow through the entire curriculum, enriching the writing of poetry and prose, from music and movement to the way in which the child arrives at solutions to problems and presents his ideas.

Does this all sound too idealistic? Whatever our gifts as a class-teacher we cannot look at a class in isolation from the school of which it is a part. Excellent facilities and well-trained manpower are of little worth if teaching methods are unco-ordinated; for the child is continually developing in mind and body as he moves through the school from 4 plus to 12. Thus it is essential that the staff be united by common ideals, purposes and philosophy, bound by the belief that the curriculum is broad, unfettered by subject considerations and trite, meaningless educational phrases; that it is *children* we teach, not *subjects*.

But can teachers teach, can children learn without a timetable, without a curriculum? I have always felt the need for some sort of structure for the day but I do not believe that this need be anything more than a rough map indicating direction, which can be amended (or scrapped) as required to meet the needs of particular children or groups attempting specific activities. I cannot accept that there is any point in a minute by minute breakdown of the day into set periods to meet the supposed requirements of 'The Office' and its band of inspectors (who prowl the division ready to pounce on any poor probationer who is doing 'art' in a 'maths' period). Indeed the majority of advisers are more interested in children and what they are doing than in paper plans.

And the curriculum . . . ? There is nothing more certain to start a heated discussion among teachers than to question the validity of the traditional curriculum. I make this point strongly because what we teach will to some extent determine how we teach, i.e. a truly creative approach to the curriculum will be difficult to implement if it is hedged round with text books which need to be studied and a whole series of facts which have to be learned. This rigidity of subject-content and presentation is more marked in schools in the United States (where the grade system prevails) than in the majority of schools in this country. Let us merely note that creative work – in which the children are given a degree of freedom of approach to learning –

1. Fairground. Group picture 72″ × 30″. Nine and ten year olds. Powder colour.

2. Christopher (aged 9) makes pirates from fabric.

3. . . . and stuffed animals from paper scraps.

4. A space probe from a cardboard tube (8 year old).

is more difficult to get under way if child and teacher are enmeshed in a formal syllabus and an inelastic timetable.

This brings us to the point in the day which is fixed as though it were the one sacred feature of school life – playtime. I read recently of the furore caused by a teacher who proclaimed *in public* that the worst aspect of the Primary School today was the sight of children huddling in windswept groups in a bleak asphalt playground on a winter afternoon. Why have a formal playtime at all? Many schools are now attempting to work an 'integrated day' as a solution to this problem.

Having worked an integrated programme for several years I am not sure that I really understand the term. Does it mean, in the words of Heraclitus, 'Everything flows, nothing is fixed' or does it imply a learning situation which does not disintegrate half-hourly? I see an integrated day as one in which the curriculum is not needlessly broken down into quite unrelated subjects, where child is not for ever separated from child because of inequality of age, sex or intelligence, where play and learning run so imperceptibly side by side that there is no desire for formal breaks – where the child separates himself from the restrictions of school and becomes for a moment little more than a leaping, jumping, screaming animal within the confines of the playground – a day in which teacher and taught do not live apart on different planes in the same world, a day which provides outlets for the whole child – emotionally, creatively, intellectually, spiritually. The school should, of course, be orderly, for children need a pattern of living which they both understand and can follow; but this pattern must not be so fragmented that it is impossible to establish a meaningful unity in the whole business of learning. 'The whole must become more significant than the organisation of the parts, for form and shape must be given to the welter of incoherent fragments that enter our experience.'

I am not living in cloud-cuckoo-land when I suggest that these 'playtimes' – often the first thing written on a new timetable – are quite unrelated to teaching or learning. I appreciate that if teachers are asked to work a day of this sort, where formal play periods and lunch times are blurred by the working programme, certain things will be lost, such as daily staff get-togethers over coffee, regular 'playtime' practices of football, netball and cricket teams, those few minutes of peace for teacher and taught when each can get away from the other. Nor am I unaware that certain new problems arise. Who, for example, is responsible in the legal sense for a child playing cricket outside with a small group when the teacher is still indoors listening to backward readers? Auxiliaries and teachers' aides would be a very useful addition to the teaching force in this respect.

All that I have written so far about timetables, play and curricula emphasises that there is nothing more alien to young children than the adult concept of time. Many of our schools fail because time is made to reign supreme – so many minutes per day being spent on mental arithmetic tables, English grammar, geography, nature study, history and so on. When a child is en-

8

grossed in any topic – whether it be the diameter of a circle, Norman England, Beethoven's music, de la Mare's poetry or setting up a loom, time is irrelevant. If we accept that the curriculum should be thought of in terms of 'activity and experience rather than of knowledge to be acquired and facts to be stored'[1] then we should give thought to how best the child can spend his time at school. Successful creative work can only come when the child is free to work for as long (or as short) as he is able. It is no good, for example, encouraging a child to begin an exacting piece of work and when he is deeply involved in it telling him to put it away because he must do another English exercise or prepare for his practical mathematics. Some of the most valuable art and craft I have ever done with groups of children has been achieved during such periods of complete 'timelessness' – when all other things stopped because of the work in hand. Let me state quite categorically that such periods often resulted in subtle maturation of the children involved. They were often followed by equally gratifying periods of study of a more conventional nature. Marion Richardson noted that one could not turn on creativity like a tap at odd moments of the week. 'Art is not an effort of will,' she wrote, 'but an act of grace. Whenever people are sincere and free art can spring up.'

What are the practical implications of what I have said so far? Basically it means that the teacher should be able to help the children for whom he is responsible to regard school as an exciting place. Then the classroom will become a centre where the children learn to read, to write, to record, to experiment, to talk, to discuss, to search out, to question, to manipulate, to play. Sometimes the whole class will learn together, sometimes small groups will be the most satisfactory unit, more often it will be the individual child who will require help, encouragement and advice. If we tackle the problems of learning in this way – 'providing great chunks of material rather than twenty minute snippets of information' – then syllabus and timetable will tend to be forgotten in the joyful experience of learning. There must of course be some fixed points in the day (eg use of the hall, TV and radio programmes, assembly, music) although it is worth recording that in Sybil Marshall's stimulating book *Experiment in Education* even these fixed points were extremely flexible (mainly because in a one-teacher village school all the things mentioned above are already practiced).

The simplest way of coming to terms with this problem is to have at least one group of children engaged in some form of graphic art or modelling. This means that once a piece of work has begun it can be completed by allowing the child to experiment and to develop powers of concentration which might otherwise have lain dormant. This graphic group work on a rota system allows each child to have one or two large blocks of painting time per month rather than a series of short isolated lessons. It also means that the art lesson does not degenerate into a period when we all paint snowmen

[1] *Handbook of Suggestions for Teachers in Primary Schools*. HMSO. 1959

or the harvest festival 'to be finished next week' when the inclination and inspiration have usually evaporated.[1]

This freer approach to art and craft – allowing it to become an integral part of learning instead of a window dressing – can lead to much less compartmentalisation in other subjects, for the art group may use their time to link up with environmental studies, number projects or to illustrate themes in poetry and literature. This 'unity of learning' has to some extent developed side by side with discoveries in the field of Gestalt psychology. No longer need we try to break down learning into isolated topics but should try to deal with the child's work as a whole.

There are any number of ways in which an integrated programme can be initiated – the particular method adopted will largely be determined by the teacher's personal philosophy and the physical limitations of the building. Obviously a teacher fortunate enough to be employed in a school designed by the Department of Education and Science Development group will find it easier to work a completely free day than one labouring in a building erected by the Fabians in the 1880s.

At one school in which I taught, the junior day followed the pattern of the infants' department (which lived in the same building). Each morning began with assembly followed by a ninety minute activity period in which the children did individual or group work of their choice. This gave opportunities for the teacher to be free to help individual children with specific difficulties – in reading, number, craft or environmental studies. During this time, the school library was manned by fourth year children. This meant that younger members of the school community could be helped to look up information – a vital part of purposeful learning. The activity period was followed by work of a rather more traditional nature – with timetable periods for hall and radio. (This did not mean that the hall, film strip darkroom or radio were never used during the first period of the day. The great value of an integrated day is the flexibility it gives.) The last twenty minutes of each day were spent discussing with the children the activities they would attempt on coming to school next morning. Often it was a continuation of the work previously begun; from time to time a whole new project would emerge from some topic which had been discussed during the day. 'Could we not make that experiment apparatus from the radio leaflet?' 'That history model I started – Jean, Peter . . . , want to help with the houses. I've got enough boxes. All right, sir?' This talking, planning and discussion is as important a part of learning as actually sitting down doing the activity.

Can any of us do anything well without giving some thought to it?

[1] For a detailed analysis of this method see *Creative Art and Craft* by H. Pluckrose. Macdonald. Second Edition 1969.

The Role of the Teacher

'Art and Craft are one, involving different ways of approaching the same human activity and expressing the same deep-rooted urge to give visible form to ideas engendered by contact with the world around us.'

Vera Rambant

In the preceding chapter I mentioned the study that Professor Torrance of the University of Minnesota has made of the creative process. His work suggests (among other things) that educators in the past have devoted far too much time and effort to learning, too little to thinking; for 'if teaching is to be effective it must contain a creative element' (here I am reminded of Mark Twain's remark that 'Education consists mainly of what we have unlearned'). While many teachers in Britain would perhaps question the purpose of tests to measure 'creativity' and to obtain a creativity 'score', the work being done in American schools and universities at least suggests that the whole question of teaching method and content is under review (a strange observation this, when the American elementary school appears to be far more rigid in structure of curriculum and subject presentation than the most formal Primary School in this country).

All that has been said so far would suggest that creativity – invention with spontaneity and imagination – flourishes in an environment where the needs and aptitudes of the child are regarded as of paramount importance. But we must not allow this to be an excuse for thoughtless, sloppy teaching. Of course there will be a time when the children need guidance – how best to obtain heavy layers of impasto on a seascape or how to punctuate a piece of free writing. The point to remember is that it is as useless to make John paint with a knife as an academic exercise as it is for him to repunctuate a passage from Dickens when he can barely read or write. Our teaching and, therefore, the children's learning (which after all is the same process seen from opposite viewpoints) will be more purposeful if it is related to the needs of the child at his particular stage of development.

Thus creative activities at Primary School level – the main concern of this book – should be based on the children's desire to enquire into how materials behave. Egg shells and cartons, string and sand, paper bags and plastic sheeting are therefore as challenging creatively as acrylics, balsa wood, leather or cane. All art tends to contain an element of the accidental, spontaneous inspiration flowing from the activity itself. In my experience children place much greater emphasis and gain more from the activity than on the production and use of the finished product. 'I've painted my model; can I try that plaster stuff?'

In *The Biology of Art*, by Desmond Morris, an attempt is made to relate the drawings of the higher apes with the early scribbles of childhood. It is interesting to note that one of the things discovered from the research was that the chimps became engrossed in the lines made by brush and pain that they did not need rewards to encourage them to complete their picture. The most significant part of the work for teachers, however, is the implica tion that young children tend to experiment by drawing shapes – circles straight lines, boxes and cubes, curves and dots – until quite accidentally recognisable pattern of shape emerges. Observing nursery children at wor with picture-making materials is fascinating in this respect. The pictur often begins as a few daubs of brightly coloured lines and as more and mor are made the subject changes miraculously from a postman, to a house i the park until, finally satisfied, the child proclaims 'That's Mrs. Smith i prayers and there's her piano.' A variety of unconventional material available to older children will mean this type of extremely valuable ex perimental picture-making can be continued throughout the impressionabl years of childhood.

Successful creative work also stems from experiences gained outside th confines of the classroom for 'the aim of the school should be to extend th world'. Visits to museums and galleries, churches, castles and stately home will provide background material for acting out situations, research i books and leaflets, writing and recording, drawing and sketching. To stan on the top of a Norman keep fires the imagination far more than any picture to run up the slopes of a Celtic hillfort like Maiden Castle in Dorset will re create the problems overcome by Vespasian when storming it better tha any contemporary account. Handling the books in a chained library, touch ing misericords carved by a mediaeval craftsman and seeing John Piper' windows in Coventry Cathedral will all help to make the arts relevant in a age of built-in obsolescence, cheap plastics and indifferent craftsmanship.

Experiences outside the classroom such as those mentioned above will mean that other subjects in the curriculum can be enriched, integrated or pulled together into a meaningful whole. Subject specialisation is completely foreign to childhood. Many progressive mathematics books, for example, present number within a framework of historical development, social con vention and practical need rather than as an enclosed topic which bears no relationship to any other aspect of the school curriculum.

Moreover let us never forget that art and craft provide a valuable therapy, a means of easing the frustrations of our industrial society, when self-expression and sensitivity are steadily losing ground. John Ciardi, the American poet, writes, 'An ulcer, gentlemen, is an unkissed imagination taking its revenge for having been jilted. It is an unwritten poem, a neglected music, an unpainted water colour, an undanced dance. It is a declaration from the mankind of man that a clear spring of joy has not been tapped and that it must break through muddily on its own.'

From all of this it must be obvious to us as teachers that when a human being is deeply involved in any piece of creative work, he is at his most sensitive – to criticism and to praise. How many of us have winced when some well-meaning adult has peered at a child whilst he is painting and

12

emarked casually 'Very nice John. What's it supposed to be?' J. C. Hill, n Inspector in North-East London between the wars, wrote that before ny work could progress the teacher needed to provide 'an environment of eep tranquillity'. This implies much more than silence broken only by pen r brush on paper. It means that the teacher provides a base from which the hild can reach out and come to terms with the world, being able to express is fears and frustrations, joys, enthusiasms and make-believes in prose and oetry, paint and clay, music and mime – or whatever mode of self-ex-ression is right for him at that particular moment in his development. 'If reativity is not to be thwarted, freedom to express is essential in those vital arly years at school for their (the children's) creative power will either levelop or atrophy.' (*The Growth of Child Art* by R. Tomlinson and J. Mills, ULP.)

But theories are all very well – classroom practice can often be a very lifferent matter. There are few children in our classes who come into school ach morning overflowing with ideas in writing, movement, painting and craft. (The great surge towards a more liberal approach to learning immedi-tely after the last war foundered because the line between freedom and icence became blurred and the role of the teacher confused.) Nowadays ur task is to provide an environment in which every child's innate abilities nd skills are developed to the full and this is almost impossible to achieve vithout stimulation from a mature, lively, adult mind.[1]

To inspire and stimulate for forty weeks of the year forty young develop-ng minds is a fearsome demand to make upon the resources of any solitary idult! Yet although there can be no one method of approach to suit all eachers and all children at all times, there are some avenues along which it s more profitable to travel than others.

Music is an excellent means of stimulating children since it provides a starting point for writing, movement and the arts. Listening to music, particularly if it can be backed by an exciting story, is a certain way of firing he enthusiasm of even the dullest child. Care should be taken in selecting he excerpts which (initially at any rate) should be short and dramatic. The ape recorder is valuable here because the passages can be taped, thus allow-ing the teacher to concentrate on the story rather than in finding the appro-priate groove. If it is possible to introduce the music to the children in some other way before it is used in the classroom so much the better (eg Assembly – which should provide moments of peaceful, undistracted listening).

When the story has been told and the music discussed and commented upon by the children it is best not to follow up immediately with a lesson involving written work, painting or movement, for the music must be allowed to occupy a place in the curriculum in its own right.

Here I am not concerned with the Dotheboys Hall approach to practical learning: 'We go upon the practical mode of teaching, Nickleby; the regular education system. C-l-e-a-n, clean, verb active, to make bright, to scour. W-i-n-d-e-r, winder, a casement, When a boy knows this out of a book, he goes and does it.'

Initially I select records which can also be used for movement. A child who has actually moved, for example, like a broom will be much more able to paint a picture of such a scene from the Sorcerer's Apprentice or write about the feelings of the young would-be magician; a group who have made a wave pattern with their bodies to Wagner's 'Flying Dutchman' are more likely to express the feelings of a rough sea in paint. Those readers who have followed Glynn Harris's excellent radio series 'Music, movement and mime with painting and writing will know from experience how much more lively the children's creative work tends to be. It is worth remembering that every child will be more able to express things he has experienced than flights of pure fantasy and imagination. Moreover the discipline imposed by the music will often provide a balanced outlet for the rich, imaginative life which is one of the chief characteristics of the Primary School child. Recorded music, sounds and rhythms used wisely will not only provide the basis for a great variety of movement but as the starting point for a whole variety of inter-related creative activities – poetry, painting and prose.

Let me illustrate this with an example. Penelope, a ten-year-old of average ability, always enjoyed listening to music and invariably became deeply in-volved in imaginative mime. After listening to 'The Witches' Sabbath' from Berlioz' *Symphonie Fantastique* she gathered a group of children around her and prepared a mime to a short extract of the music. Some of the group used this experience for picture making, others for puppets. Not so Penelope. Instead of painting or modelling she wrote 'I sit there in the tree, tense, watching strange shapes gather in the clearing. The shapes are tall and thin, slow moving round their cauldrons. Suddenly one jumps above the others and begins to jig about very strangely, slyly. She wears a black robe. Her eyes are cruel and cold, her hair matted. Her thin voice calls the dead from the earth. She has no friends but her owl, her cat and her cauldron. Such is the life of a witch.'

Writing such as this, displayed with paintings or mounted in a class anthology, helps to pull together the curriculum, at the same time giving the children a unity of purpose and of learning. The writing flows from the movement, the movement into painting and modelling. This experience can be extended by exploring other people's interpretations of similar happenings. My example here could be deepened and extended through the poetry of Walter de la Mare (*My Great Grand Dam, The Listeners*); Grieg's *Peer Gynt Suite*, Mussorgsky's tone poem *The Hut of Baba-Yaga*; the prose of John Masefield (*The Midnight Folk, The Box of Delights*) and Sir Arthur Grimble ('The Limping Man of Makin Meang' from *A Pattern of Islands*).

This type of work obviously requires careful preparation on the part of the teacher. It necessitates a breadth of reading and listening which must be backed up by a sound knowledge of children – when to supply more momen-tum through music and verse and when to change the topic completely.

Having inspired work along particular lines and given the children the opportunity to develop their interests within the broad framework of the

14

heme under consideration, the teacher has another equally important task.
s work is finished it will need to be attractively presented, for display
hould be an integral part of modern educational practice.

Let me say straight away that I am not advocating fabric drapes for the
ake of fabric drapes nor the odd pot on a shelf simply as an eye-catching
immick. If display is to be meaningful it should surely aim at making the
hildren's work look as attractive as possible and at the same time emphasise
ny relevant points which were learned during the study. This educational
ontent will obviously be of interest to other children in the school who were
ot engaged in the work as well as to other members of staff and parents.

It is difficult to define a 'good display' – for this is essentially a visual ex-
erience. Shape balances shape, the colours selected harmonise with each
ther, there is a feeling of space and yet an overall feeling of unity. Such
hings are felt – not written about. Yet there are some points which can be
nade because they are not based upon ephemeral qualities like those listed
bove.

(1) Do we always leave our display boards plain or do we cover them
vith some form of lining paper to add extra colour to the classroom? All
orts of papers are suitable – coloured sugar paper, pastel, wall paper, tissue;
he one chosen should be determined by the type of work which is to be
nounted upon it. A yellow pastel paper makes an attractive backing for
fire' pictures, deep blue for snow scenes. Fabric lengths can also be used
ccasionally to add variety. Fabrics like crash, hessian and imitation linen
which have a coarse weave or a heavy slub are particularly valuable for this
purpose.

(2) Do we trim the childrens' work and mount it on paper before we display it? Children's paintings often look tatty round the edges and it only
takes a little effort to make them look really fresh and new.

(3) How do we mount the pictures, written extracts, word lists, book
jackets? Do we just stick them up and hope that they are reasonably eye-
catching? Do we use great brass pins for the smallest of pictures or do we
prefer to use staple guns, rampins (Dryad supply both) and mapping pins,
so that *what* is shown is more easily noticed than *how* it is held up? Study
the window display of a large store and see how pertinent this point is.

(4) How much thought do we give to making sure that the overall effect
of our classroom is not one of rigid formality? Need all the pictures be in
straight lines level with the Victorian picture rail?

Now all this might seem quite irrelevant in a book on creative themes
and the thought of teachers spending their time trimming and mounting
might well make some readers feel that I am stressing quite the wrong things.
It is important, however, that we treat the childrens' work with respect and
care. Forty wet pictures, dripping with paint, thrown on top of a cupboard
on Friday to be torn apart and distributed the next week to be finished is
hardly going to make children feel that their work is of much value; pinning
the best two crooked on the classroom door will merely confirm this feeling.

It is also worth remembering that children spend a great deal of their day in the classroom and because of this it is our duty to make the room as attractive as we possibly can. I would go so far as to say that the poorer the childrens' home backgrounds are the more vital this duty becomes (a singular fact – but it is in these twilight areas that teachers are at a premium!)

I think the general care we lavish on a classroom will be reflected in time in the way children present their work, and in the respect they show for other peoples' work and other peoples' property (be it paint brushes, reading books, models, hats or coats).

The Plowden Report makes all the points I have made above – much more succintly and with greater emphasis.

'We should like to see the schools becoming, much more than most of them now are, places in which children are surrounded by many examples, old and new, of taste and discrimination – furniture, clocks, ceramics, pictures and books . . . Much of the beauty in the school environment should be created by the children themselves and by the care taken in the display of their work. There are schools which already do much and which are showing others the way. Though opportunities and circumstances are very unequal, every school could do something and in the aggregate the schools could become a strong, perhaps a decisive influence on public taste.' (Paragraph 685).

Thus I would suggest that it is no good paying lip service to the provision of a creative environment and little real purpose in giving children great chunks of lively purposeful learning if the end product is not going to make them feel proud of an interesting and exciting task well done. 'Look, this is what we learned; this display is our method of presenting our knowledge to you.'

FAIRGROUNDS AND MARKETS

Fairgrounds and Markets

The fairground: an evocative title even for grown-ups. The fairground full of magic, rich in colour, a place which is exciting, noisy, restless. The very nature of the fairground, allied to the fact that most children will have had some direct experience of fairs, means that here is a subject which will appeal to all age groups from the ebullient five-year-old to the sophisticated teenager.

I usually introduce the theme through music which will quickly conjure up memories of the side-shows and the jostling crowds – conveyed admirably in the first few minutes of Stravinsky's music to the ballet, *Petrouchka*. have used this record as the background for straightforward accounts of a fairground (with less able ten-year-olds) to mimed passages from Diaghilev's ballet story. Here again the opening four minutes of the music provide opportunity for a range of movement. The ballet begins with scene in the great square of St. Petersburg. It is Shrove Tuesday in the year 1830. Holiday-makers, rich and poor, young and old, jostle round the side shows; there are tumblers and fortune tellers, tradesmen selling cloth vegetables and charms, while a hurdy-gurdy man plays a street organ on which a monkey dances. There is a drum beat. A puppet-master sets up his side-show. He is, unknown to the wondering audience, a magician, and his three puppets Petrouchka, the Moor and the Dancer are almost human The rest of the story – in which the brutal Moor kills Petrouchka – can be omitted. In movement the class could mime the scene in the square – each child working individually as a stall-holder, a tumbler or an interested passer-by. This leads to group work, some children buying and selling others watching the tumblers or listening to the hurdy-gurdy man's music When the puppet man appears there is the possibility of building even larger group shapes as everybody gathers round the theatre to watch the puppet show.

When I use this as a theme I occasionally let the children speak as well as mime. This adds another dimension to the experience. Usually, however, save this for after-school drama work when the resulting noise (a fairground, after all, is noisy) will not bother teachers working on more sedentary topics Another excellent dance form can result from asking the children to mime a marionette to the beautiful lilting music of the first recognisable theme in the opening section.

The fair at St. Petersburg is some way from a fair on Hampstead Heath but the spirit behind both is similar. If the story outlined above is used in any depth, writing and picture making will stem naturally from the music – but it is equally possible for Stravinsky's music to be used for a mime set in modern Birmingham or Edinburgh.

There is comparatively little poetry about fairgrounds in anthologies I have studied, although gipsies and similar wandering folk are to be found in

18

profusion. These vary from the romantic ('Where he comes from nobody knows, Nor where he goes to, but on he goes.' *The Pedlar's Caravan.*) to beautifully drawn word pictures full of atmosphere ('the old wives puffed their pipes nigh as black as their hair' – Edmund Blunden, *The Idlers*). Poems of this latter type are excellent starting points both for painting and writing. Teachers of secondary children (or bright fourth year juniors) might also introduce an extract from William Cowper's *The Task* (*The Sofa*, lines 571-574). Traditional songs and ballads might also be used. There are a great number of these, such as *Strawberry Fair, The Old Woman who Lost her Petticoats, Widdicombe Fair, Trotting to the Fair*.

Interesting research into local fairs is worth while. Many of these go back to mediaeval times when merchants travelled from France and the Netherlands as well as from the outlying parts of the British Isles to buy and sell. An interesting account of fairs (with details of royal charters, pie powder courts and the like) is to be found in Christina Hole's *English Custom and Usage*, (Batsford). A fascinating description of a jostling market is to be found in Henry Mayhew's *London Labour and the London Poor* in the section headed 'The London street market on a Saturday night'. 'Here is a stall glittering with new tin saucepans. There another bright with blue and yellow crockery and sparkling with white glass. One man shows off his yellow haddock with a candle stuck in a bundle of firewood.'

Much worthwhile art work can stem from this theme. Whether it is to be used for individual picture-making or large group murals it is important to encourage the children to talk about their last visit to a fairground. This will help them to recall their own individual experiences thus helping make the paintings which follow upon the discussion more personal and vivid. This sharing of common ground will also help the diffident child by giving him the opportunity of drawing upon the ideas of his more extrovert contemporaries.

What sort of things will be discussed? The setting of the local fairground will colour the whole picture. Is it rural, like the fairs held on Peckham Rye or Harpenden Common, or very commercial, like Southend Kursaal or Butlin's at Clacton? Are we to portray the fairground at night (when resist techniques using Freart crayons and ebony stain will be especially suitable) or to attempt to recapture the atmosphere of an August bank holiday afternoon? Is it our aim to paint a particular stall or fairground showman or to record the whole fairground – caravans, swings, big dipper and all? Older children will benefit from discussions along these lines and they could profitably be extended by asking them to think about the feelings we experience when sitting in the big wheel, in a dodgem car or rushing down the water shute. Can these feelings be recaptured in paint or pencil? If so, how? In this connection photographs cut from newspapers and periodicals will prove useful. The camera can catch the odd angle and this will often lead children to the realisation that for effect and dramatic impact the artist (like the photographer) could well try to present his ideas from an unusual viewpoint. If the photographs are of no great value they could be mounted on frieze to make a fairground collage when the discussion period has ended The pictures are cut up, the subjects being regrouped to give a unity to th whole design.

All of these are ways in which the child can freely express himsel Whether he uses paint, card, clay, movement or words, the result is in vention and spontaneity, which after all is what creativity is all about.

Music

Composer	Title of work
Berlioz	Overture – *Roman Carnival*
Coates	'Covent Garden' *London Suite*
Debussy	*Fêtes Galantes*
Delius	*Brigg Fair*
Dvorák	*Second overture, Carnival*
Elgar	Overture – *Cockaigne*
German	Incidental music (dances) to *Henry VIII* and *Nell Gwynne*
Grainger	*Mock Morris*
	Shepherd's Hay
Haydn	Finale of Symphony No. 82 in C, *The Bear*
Quilter	*Three English Dances*
Ravel	'Feria' from *Rapsodie Espagnole*
Respighi	Orchestral suite, *Roman Festivals*
Smetana	'The Acrobats' – *The Bartered Bride*
Stravinsky	*Circus Polka*

Poetry

Descriptive

Anon	*The Old Market Woman*
	Scarborough Fair
Walter de la Mare	*All the Fun*
Thomas Hardy	*Sheep Fair*
James Reeves	*Street Musician*
Kenneth Slessor	'In and out the country folk' (from *Carnival Music*)

Historical

Terence Tiller	*Street Performers 1851*
Traditional	*Street Cries of London*

Humorous

William Plomer	*The Caledonian Market*

Lyrical

W. B. Rands	*Pedlar's Caravan*
Clive Sansom	*The Roundabout*
Shakespeare	*The Winter's Tale* (Act IV, Scene 4)

Narrative

Anon	*Wraggle Taggle Gipsies*
	Strawberry Fair
	Widdecombe Fair
	Sledburn Fair
	Oh, Dear! What Can The Matter Be
	Fine Knacks for Ladies
Patrick R. Chalmers	*Roundabouts and Swings*

ANIMALS

Animals

There are very few children who are not fascinated by animals. This interest is quickly apparent if children are allowed to produce study books on subjects of their own choice – animal projects are invariably the most popular. This generalisation seems to apply equally to town and country children and even in schools where few classroom pets are kept.

This innate interest in animals can become a source of a great variety of written work. Moreover, if the children's first-hand knowledge is extended by poetry and music (and visits to zoos and museums) then the total experience of the group will be deepened even further.

When embarking on this topic I find it best to begin by discussing with the group the characteristics, appearance and habits of a domestic animal . . . a cat, a dog or a rabbit. This discussion is supplemented with prose readings or poetry so that the selected animal is presented in as many different moods as possible (obviously we like a cat much more when it is curled up in front of a fire than when it is savagely tearing a blackbird to pieces). As there are as many ways of developing this theme as there are animals to write about, I will restrict myself in this instance to cats. By doing this I can indicate an approach which could be applied with equal success to other animals.

Introduce the subject by playing 'The Song of the Jellicles' (from T. S. Eliot's *Practical Cats*, spoken by Robert Donat, music by Alan Rawsthorne). If this is not obtainable use 'The Song of the Cats' from Ravel's *L'Enfant et les Sortilèges* (opening 3 minutes of the second side). Follow this with readings selected from:

Walter de la Mare	*Five Eyes*
T. S. Eliot	*Old Possum's Book of Practical Cats*
Eleanor Farjeon	*Cat-Scat*
Ted Hughes	*Esther's Tomcat*
Edward Lear	*The Owl and the Pussy Cat*
Don Marquis	*The Tom Cat*
Christopher Smart	'Cat Jeoffrey' (from *Jubilate*)
Stevie Smith	*The Singing Cat*
A. S. J. Tessimond	*Cats*
Edward Thomas	*A Cat*

As in most other learning situations much will depend upon how well the teacher prepares the ground – an insensitive preparation invariably leads to stolid uninspired writing. I usually remind the children before they begin to write that I am more concerned with feelings than spellings. We can always correct spellings and (if it is necessary) the child can always make a fair copy of his work.

I suppose the thing which gives us most concern is the standard the children attain and the difficulty we experience when attempting to evaluate their work. What, I sometimes wonder, would a teacher of the 1920s make of the piece of work which follows, written by an eight-year-old?

> When it is night you
> Cannot see a cat.
> All you can see
> Are two green balls.
> When you go to grab him
> He melts away into the dark.

Not all animals are as appealing as cats, however, and it is often revealing to ask the group to comment upon creatures they dislike or even fear. D. H. Lawrence's description of *Man and the Bat* resulted in the following:

> A dragon fly in my shoe
> A huge creepy dragon fly
> The thing came out of my shoe
> And onto my shoulder.
> I tried to kill it.
> But no´
> It flew away onto the door
> I tried again to kill it
> I hit it with my hand
> As it fell its legs seemed to dance
> Then it stopped
> Its legs were still
> It was dead.

(written by a boy of 8 years 6 months, who was really describing an incident with a crane fly or Daddy-Long-Legs).

Picture-making in paint, paper and crayon can be linked to the children's writings, poems and prose extracts. Pictures and writing mounted together make attractive displays – particularly if photographs of animals and selected lines from the children's favourite poems are included. Reproductions of the work of the following artists will also be useful – Delacroix, de Hondecoeter, Hicks, Kuhnert, Landseer, Marc, Munnings, Moreland, Scott, Stubbs.

If the theme is to be linked to work in movement the music of cats from Ravel's musical play (see above) is excellent both for individual mime of 'cats at night' and for work in pairs of 'cats at play'.

Music

Composer	Title of work
Britten	*Noye's Fludde*
Coates	Suite, *The Three Bears*
Daquin	*Le Coucou*
Debussy	*Poissons d'Or* (*Images*, 2nd set, No. 3)
Delius	*On hearing the First Cuckoo*
Granados	*The Maiden and the Nightingale*
Grieg	*Papillon* (Lyric pieces, 1886)
Haydn	*The Creation* extracts, e.g. 'The Worm'
Harty	*With the Wild Geese*
Mussorgsky	'Hatching Chicks' from *Pictures at an Exhibition*
Prokofiev	*Peter and the Wolf*
Rimsky-Korsakov	*The Golden Cockerel*
	The Flight of the Bumble Bee
Rossini	*The Thieving Magpie*
Saint-Saëns	*Carnival of Animals*
Schubert	*The Trout*
Sibelius	*The Swan of Tuonela*
Smetana	*The Little Hen* (Bohemian Dances, No. 2)
Stravinsky	*The Firebird*
Tchaikovsky	'The Dance of the little Swans' from *Swan Lake*
Vaughan Williams	*The Lark Ascending*
	The Wasps

Poetry

Descriptive

Walter de la Mare	*Nicholas Nye*
	Five Eyes
G. K. Chesterton	*The Donkey*
Ted Hughes	*View of a Pig*
Don Marquis	*The Tom Cat*
Edith Sitwell	*Madam Mouse Trots*
Robert Louis Stevenson	*The Cow*
A. S. J. Tessimond	*Cats*
Edward Thomas	*A Cat*

Historical

Ralph Hodgson	*The Bells of Heaven*
Milton	'The Sixth Day' from *Paradise Lost*
Clive Sansom	*The Donkey's Owner*

Humorous

Hilaire Belloc	*Cautionary Tales*
Patrick Barrington	*I Had a Hippopotamus*
Walter de la Mare	*The Ship of Rio*
T. S. Eliot	*Old Possum's Book of Practical Cats*
F. W. Harvey	*Ducks*
Edward Lear	*The Owl and the Pussy Cat*
A. A. Milne	*The Dormouse and the Doctor*
Ogden Nash	*The Porcupine*
James Reeves	*Prefabulous Animiles*
Theodore Roethke	*The Lady and the Bear*

Lyrical

William Blake	*The Lamb*
	The Tyger
W. H. Davies	*Leisure*
Walter de la Mare	*Earth Folk*
Fiona Macleod	*Lone Dog*
V. Sackville-West	*Greater Cats*

Mystery

'Banjo' Paterson	*Waltzing Matilda*
Edwina Muir	*The Animals*
	The Combat
Louis Untermeyer	*Leviathan*

Narrative

Anon	*The Crocodile*
	The Fox
R. H. Barham	*The Jackdaw of Rheims*
John Clare	*The Badger*
Clifford Dyment	*Hedgehog in an Air Raid*
Thomas Hardy	*The Oxen*
D. H. Lawrence	*Man and Bat*
	The Hummingbird
	The Snake
John Masefield	*Reynard the Fox*
Hal Summers	*The Rescue*

See also *Penguin Book of Animal Verse* edited by George MacBeth; *Four Feet and Two*, edited by Leila Berg, published by Puffin Books.

Prose Extracts

Anon	*Androcles*
	The Story of Gelert
Joy Adamson	*Born Free*
Aesop	*Fables*
David Attenborough	*Zoo Quest to Guiana*
'B.B.'	*String Lug the Fox*
	Down the Bright Stream
	The Little Grey Men
M. Batten	*The Singing Forest*
The Bible	Creation of The Animal Kingdom
	Noah
	Daniel
	The Horse (Job 39 v 19-25)
Chaucer	*The Nun's Priest's Tale*
F. Davison	*Man-shy*
Gerald Durrell	*The Bafut Beagles*
B. Evans	*Romany* Books
Paul Gallico	*The Snow Goose*
Kenneth Grahame	*The Wind in the Willows*
Sir Arthur Grimble	*A Pattern of Islands*
Joel Harris	*Uncle Remus* Books
Rudyard Kipling	*The Just So Stories*
	The Jungle Books
Jack London	*The Call of the Wild*
P. Lynch	*Long Ears the Donkey*
Gavin Maxwell	*Ring of Bright Water*
A. A. Milne	*Christopher Robin* Books
Liam O' Flaherty	*The Seagull* (short stories)
A. Seaby	*Skewbald the New Forest Pony*
E. Seton	*Lives of the Hunted Wild Animals I Have Known*
Anna Sewell	*Black Beauty*
J. H. Williams	*Elephant Bill*
Henry Williamson	*Tarka the Otter*

MAGIC + FANTASY

Magic and Fantasy

All in a hot and copper sky
The bloody sun at noon
Right up above the mast did stand
No bigger than the moon
The very deep did rot: O Christ
That ever this should be!
Yea slimy things did crawl with legs
Upon the slimy sea.

I have chosen this excerpt from Samuel Taylor Coleridge's *Rime of the Ancient Mariner* because it illustrates clearly how poetry (provided it is carefully selected and well read) can be used to fire the children's imagination, making them want to talk, to write, to model, to paint, to act. If the story is chosen with care, if it is out of the ordinary, we are more likely to get work from the group which is not commonplace. Do we challenge the children enough? I know, for example, that my maths teaching lacks 'flair'. I am sure that the children I work with, given a teacher committed to and understanding the implications of the Nuffield project would be much more alive mathematically than they are at present. I am equally certain, however, that there are many classes who go through junior school on a much more sterile diet than does mine when it comes to paint and crayon, poetry and music. Thus I would suggest that we do not necessarily need to 'stretch' the children by filling them with a vast quantity of facts. Far more important are the experiences which the school can provide – school journeys, visits to theatres, concert halls, art galleries and museums; music and poetry, prose and drama, science and mathematics, environmental studies and art presented as though they were relevant to them as people.

This philosophy will, of course, affect even the most mundane aspects of school life – such as buying equipment and books. Is there any point, for example, in buying class sets of poetry anthologies when the class that is given them will probably be stimulated by less than a quarter of the contents. I make this point because the poems I mention in this series are not to be found in any one 'teacher's omnibus' – indeed some of my suggestions for readings may not appeal to every teacher. Surely one of our first tasks in our attempt to provide an atmosphere in which creative work will flourish is to build up our own anthology (or to use A. P. Wavell's expression our own 'ragbag') into which we can dip when the occasion arises.

I have already touched upon the possibility of using a theme based on magic or fantasy as the starting point for creative work. This need not be restricted to the traditional magicians and witches of our fairy stories but can embrace the whole world of make-believe (which, after all, plays a very real part in the young child's progress towards maturity). It is essential to provide an outlet for day-dreams, for to give shape to imagination is to come to terms with it. Is this not art therapy at its most rudimentary level?

But there is another equally important reason for occasionally selecting a 'fantastic' topic for a piece of creative work. Many of the children we teach will have experienced great difficulty in expressing in line, in movement, in words conventional everyday things – like window-cleaner, tree, fish. Let me be more explicit. If we are to paint 'window-cleaner' we must use conventional images that all can understand – ladder, bucket, man in jeans, leather, window pane, water. Imagine how a ten-year-old must feel when he has desperately wanted to record facts such as these on paper since his days in the reception class – and has continually failed. Is it any wonder that art, which is a means of communication, atrophies and dies? Thus we must provide topics which allow the children's imagination completely free play. An excellent starting point for such activities is provided in many of the poems of Edward Lear. What does a Quangle Wangle look like? No member of the group could paint a bad Quangle – each would be quite unique, a perfect representation for the child who painted it. (This particular poem is rich in weird characters – the Dong, the Olympian Bear, the Fimble Fowl with a corkscrew leg, the Attey Squash, the Bisky Bat.)

A successful method of working is to let each child paint or draw a picture arising from the poem and then write a short descriptive piece about it. Children who cannot write fluently could record a description on tape. Gifted children might prefer to present their piece of written work from a different angle. Thus, to continue with the example from Lear, 'Conversation Pieces' could be written by the creatures who come to live in the hat or a group diary made in which each character records his daily adventures.

Other poems by Edward Lear which could be used in a similar way for picture-making and writing include:

The Owl and the Pussy Cat
The Jumblies
The Nutcrackers and the Sugar Tongs
The Broom, the Shovel, the Poker, the Tongs
The Dong
The Akond of Swat
The Yonghy Bonghy Bo

(All these poems – together with the Limericks, Alphabets and short stories – are to be found in the *Complete Nonsense of Edward Lear*, edited by Holbrook Jackson, published by Faber and Faber.)

Two poems in this list (*The Nutcrackers* and *The Broom*) often fascinate the most sophisticated class. The idea of inanimate objects coming to life, having feelings or the power to communicate, is a topic which has been used by generations of teachers. But we should try to aim at a more evocative title than 'A day in the life of a Penny'.

Music will help create the mood and provide the basis for both writing and picture-making. Ravel's *L'Enfant et les Sortilèges* (recorded at present only in French) tells the story of a little boy who is thoroughly unpleasant

5. *The Ancient Mariner*
Group picture 72″ × 40″. Paint, wax crayon and fabric.

34

6. Mask-making from card (eight year old)

7. . . . from polystyrene (ten year olds).

8. Picture-making inspired by stories – Gulliver. Group work – powder colour on sugar paper 50″ × 40″ (nine and ten year olds).
Note the part which childrens' writing plays in the treatment of the topic.

9. . . . . and with acrylic paint on cotton lawn (nine and ten year olds).

and in a nightmarish dream all the things he has broken or harmed appear to haunt him – cup and saucer, chair, grandfather clock (ticking fantastically fast because of a broken pendulum), butterfly and dragon are joined by old man arithmetic and an army of numbers who come from a torn school text book. Each section of the story (to its happy ending) is clearly told in the music and several excerpts are excellent for movement; 'The Cats in the Garden' provide great scope for work in pairs (cats playing), the grandfather clock with its rapid tick for children working singly.

The music, the movement, the writing may lead naturally into group murals – the chief characters being drawn on sheets of sugar paper (15 in. × 12 in.) coloured with paint, crayon or pastel and then cut out and mounted on frieze paper.

The Sorcerer's Apprentice by Dukas (a fairy story used by Walt Disney in *Fantasia*) is also a valuable stimulus for the topic we are considering. The apprentice magician, his spell bringing the brooms to life to carry water from the well, the magician's return to find his study afloat, here are many situations suitable for drama. It is an ideal frieze subject for young children. Brooms with faces and arms (simple yet dramatic) are coloured with crayon, cut out and mounted onto a sheet of sugar paper (60 in. × 40 in.). The cut-outs should be overlapped and interlaced as they are pasted down. This will help to make the picture come alive. If the background looks a little dead, darken it with thin powder colour washes (ink or ebony stain is also effective for this). The colour – provided it has been used thinly – will be repelled by the wax cut-outs. This method of working could also be used to introduce resist techniques.

The children might also be encouraged to write the recipe for the spell. What did the apprentice have to do and say to get the brooms to obey him? How did the magician make a spell to return the water to the well? Another topic for writing can be based on the feelings of the apprentice, his joy when the brooms first begin to move, his apprehension when they will not stop, his fear on his master's return.

'The world of make-believe' is a title which fifty years ago would have been attached to the futuristic stories of H. G. Wells and Jules Verne. Yesterday's make-believes are almost today's realities. Another method, therefore, of starting children to write is to give them pictures (or draw them on the blackboard) of strange machines or photographs of common-place things taken at odd angles. Often this method of presentation will appeal to the child and stimulate his imagination.

I might well have chosen the title 'Strange Happenings' for this theme. Although we have already considered verse and prose suitable for the younger child there is a vast amount of material for the eleven to fifteen age group. With older (or more gifted) children it is often worthwhile continually to vary the presentation so that no one particular approach is followed to the exclusion of all the rest. To be more specific, *The Ancient Mariner* might be considered as a story of the sea (like *The Inchcape Rock*) or a story of retribution and eternal wandering.

There are a number of poem and prose extracts which could be used in this way.

How they are used to trigger off writing and talking depends largely upon the age of the children and the confidence they have in expressing themselves on paper. Thus some children might prefer to retell the story as though they were a character in it. Others might wish to offer an explanation for the event (eg. for the disappearance of the lighthousemen in W. W. Gibson's *Flannan Isle*). More often, however, the poem will simply build up an atmosphere which the children will incorporate in situations of their own making. Let me illustrate this. In W. W. Gibson's *The Ice Cart* the writer falls into a day-dream on his office stool, to be woken, rather unpleasantly, by the crack of the carter's whip. Stephen (aged 8) wrote this after hearing the poem.

'I was sitting on a very uncomfortable chair. We were doing sums. My chair was lifted up by an enormous wind which carried me to a castle. A loud trumpet blew and it nearly deafened me. The king of the castle shouted and I saw it was my teacher. He was shouting and waving a cane.

I got ten of the best and still had to do those sums.'

The writing should be illustrated whenever possible. The sketches provide a rich source of material for individual paintings and murals. Moreover if the drawings are included in the writing (rather than relegated to the bottom of the page and only done when all the writing is finished) the child is given the additional task of presenting a piece of work which is interesting to look at as well as interesting to read. It will encourage pride in presentation, for there is little use in being wonderfully creative if nobody wants to look at the work produced!

Music

Composer	Title of work
Arnold	*Tam O'Shanter*
Berlioz	*Symphonie Fantastique*
Britten	*The Prince and the Pagodas*
	Extracts from *Peter Grimes*
Falla	*El Amor Brujo* – 'The Magic Circle'
Grieg	*Peer Gynt* suite
	March of the Dwarfs (Lyric Suite Opus 54)
Humperdinck	*Hansel and Gretel* (extracts)
Kodály	*Háry János* suite
Mendelssohn	Incidental music to *A Midsummer Night's Dream*
Ravel	*Mother Goose* suite
Respighi	*Fountains of Rome*, second movement
Saint-Saëns	*Danse Macabre*
Sibelius	*Lemminkäinen* suite
Richard Strauss	*Till Eulenspiegel* (Symphonic poem)
Stravinsky	*The Firebird*
	The Rite of Spring
	The Soldier's Tale
Wagner	Overture to *The Flying Dutchman*
Weber	Overture to *Oberon*
Weinberger	*Schwanda the Bagpiper*
	'Schwanda's Tune'
	'Polka and Fugue'

Poetry

Descriptive

Walter de la Mare	*The Song of the Soldiers*
	The Voice
	Haunted
	Someone
	The Witch
	I saw Three Witches
	The Little Creature
Shakespeare	'Over Hill, Over Dale'
	A Midsummer Night's Dream
	'Now the Hungry Lion Roars'
	A Midsummer Night's Dream
Edith Sitwell	*Three Poor Witches*
	Ghost in the Garden
Spenser	'The Dragon' from *The Faerie Queen*

Historical

Byron	*The Destruction of Sennacherib*

Humorous

Anon	*If all the World were Paper*
Edward Lear	*The Courtship of the Yonghy Bonghy Bo*
Ogden Nash	*The Tale of Custard the Dragon*
James Reeves	*Prefabulous Animiles* (a collection of verses)
M. Stuart	*Revenant*
Thackeray	*Little Billee*

Lyrical

Walter de la Mare	*The Listeners*
Ben Johnson	*Witches' Song*
Rudyard Kipling	*The Way through the Woods*
James Reeves	*Spells*
Tennyson	*The Bugle*

Narrative

Robert Bloomfield	*The Fakenham Ghost*
Browning	*The Pied Piper*
	Childe Roland to the Dark Tower Came
Coleridge	*The Rime of the Ancient Mariner*
Walter de la Mare	*The Dwarf*
Robert Graves	*Welsh Incident*
Keats	*La Belle Dame Sans Merci*
Kingsley	*The Sands of Dee*
Tennyson	*The Lady of Shalott*

Prose

Lewis Carroll	*Alice in Wonderland*
	Alice Through the Looking Glass
Sir Arthur Conan Doyle	*The Lost World*
Henry James	*The Turn of the Screw*
C. S. Lewis	*The Lion, the Witch and the Wardrobe*
Hugh Lofting	The *Doctor Dolittle* Books
J. R. R. Tolkien	*The Hobbit*
H. G. Wells	*The Invisible Man*
	The Time Machine

Space

Space

The term space is one of the most evocative words in the young child's vocabulary. Hardly a day goes by without mention on television and in the newspaper of some startling advance in the field of space technology. Space heroes and heroines fill the comic strips, and programmes such as Dr. Who and Captain Scarlet have remained firm favourites on TV for several years.

The effect of all this on the children we teach is difficult to measure. There has been an imperceptible merging of fiction into fact. 'Spacemen' twenty years ago were creatures of the artist's imagination. Today they are scientific reality. For generations musicians and poets have used the imagery of moon and moonlight to create a feeling of wonder, magic and love. Now that spacemen can fly to the moon, how much longer will the mystery remain?

But these ever-widening scientific discoveries about our universe, backed by photographs, give shape and purpose to the child's imagination. Who knows what truths the brash pictures of our present generation of Primary School children will contain?

The point I am seeking to make is that here we have a subject for picture-making which will appeal to all children because of its relevance to life today, and because it also provides them with an opportunity to give free rein to their rich imaginations. All the time they do this, however, certain rules will be observed. 'He's got big boots on because of weightlessness on the planet', or 'I've got to paint the re-entry heat just there and I've finished'.

Where can we start? With young children the suggestion of space creatures or a lunar landscape will usually be enough to trigger off picture-making. Because the subjects are fanciful, the child who is inhibited because he cannot paint a recognisable shape is given confidence. How can anybody criticise the shape of a space cow or proclaim that a Mars horse has legs rather than wheels? (Two examples, these, from my own recent teaching experience.) One of the most exciting space pictures I have seen was entitled 'Man in the Red Moon'. Painted by a diffident seven-year-old, it was little more than a kaleidoscope of pattern and colour.

It is wise, as in every picture, to give the children choice in the shape and colour of the paper they are to use. For example, the surface of Mars will be easier to paint on crimson sugar paper than white cartridge. Older children might prefer to use their painting time to record scientific facts for a space display. These might take the form of paintings of the planets in position round the sun. More exciting (and in my opinion more worthy of the art period) is to give some of the group pictures of the moon's surface and suggest that these be used as the starting point for a painting or an abstract design. Collage-pictures, built up from all manner of junk material, are also appropriate to this older age group.

For paintings of man in space acrylic (or polymer) paints on cellophane produce unusual effects. The picture may be painted conventionally on one sheet of cellophane, or built up on several. By overlaying one sheet of cellophane on another (each sheet containing part of the picture), a feeling of depth is easily achieved. If the cellophane sheets are overlaid while the paint is still wet they will stick together. A black card frame will be necessary to give an even edge to the design.

Resist work also has a place – particularly if pictures of 'take off' are being attempted. Here the design is worked in heavy layers of wax crayon (Freart, Finart) or oil pastel on sugar paper. When finished, the drawing is given a wash of Ebony Stain (Dryad Ltd). This will stain the paper but the waxed areas will resist it. This technique is particular suited to children who draw well, but who find it difficult to paint their drawings successfully.

Group picture-making will often develop from work of the type described above. If the child's imagination is fully stimulated then we should not be surprised to find that writing, painting and model-making unite in a common 'group expression' of the experience.

In this connection music is a rich source of inspiration, for it enables children to marry together their factual knowledge with their fears and their imaginings. It gives opportunity for exotic movement and quiet listening (which in turn sparks off writing, picture-making and scientific research). For movement I use extracts from 'The Planets Suite' (Holst) and 'The Rite of Spring' (Stravinsky). Individual mimes can be based on a spaceman climbing from his capsule on a strange planet, or exploring the craters on the moon. Group work may be built around the planet itself or on space creatures and machines. 'Listening music' (though it could be used for movement equally successfully) includes the adagio sostenuto from 'The Moonlight Sonata' (Beethoven), 'On the Steppes of Central Asia' (Borodin) and much of the 'Sinfonia Antarctica' (Vaughan Williams). These pieces – though not strictly concerned with space – evoke an atmosphere of stillness and distance and as one seven-year-old put it, of 'the worlds beyond the clouds'.

Poems may be linked to the musical excerpts (one does not have to be a Burton or a Richardson to read against 'The Moonlight Sonata' with considerable effect!). There are many which take as their theme the moon and the stars but few which deal specifically with space travel. For juniors and younger seniors the following poems are particularly suitable:–

Walter de la Mare	*Silver*
Robert Graves	*Star Talk*
Gerard Manley Hopkins	*Starlight Night*
Thomas Hulme	*Above the Dock*
James Kirkup	*Tea in a Space Ship*
James Nimmo	*Space Travellers*
Sara Teasdale	*Falling Star*
Robert Louis Stevenson	*The Moon*

When the group have listened to poetry and music many of the children will be prepared to express themselves in prose and verse. Obvious starting points (walk on the moon, space creature) will often lead to fantastic flights of fantasy. One eight-year-old described how her friend was given a box of bubble bath liquid by an aunt. She then wrote 'Valerie jumped into the bath without even stopping to undress. The whole packet was in the bath, box and all. Bubbles filled the room. Soon they were big enough to climb in, which was exactly what she did. She floated away leaving a trail of bubbles all over England. Higher and higher she went. We never saw her again!'

Music

Composer	Title of work
Debussy	*Clair de Lune* (3rd movement from *Suite Bergamasque*)
Gershwin	*Rhapsody in Blue*
Haydn	Overture to *The Creation*
Holst	*The Planets*
Khatchaturian	Music to the film *Battle for Stalingrad* (1949)
Schumann	*Fantaisiestücke*, No. 2
Richard Strauss	'Elegy' from *Alpine Symphony*
	Tod und Verklärung, Part II
Stravinsky	*The Rite of Spring*

Also: electronic records (for movement, found in most gramophone catalogues)

Poetry

Descriptive

Walter de la Mare	*High*
T. E. Hulme	*Above the Dock*
G. Johnson	*The Creation*
Norman Nicholson	*Expanding Universe*
	Gathering Sticks on Sunday
Shelley	*The Moon*
Sara Teasdale	*Falling Star*
Wordsworth	'Among the Stars' (from *Peter Bell*)

Lyrical

Walter de la Mare	*Silver*
W. H. Davies	*The Moon*
	The Rainbow
Eleanor Farjeon	'The Stony Floor' (24 poems on planets and stars)
Thomas Hardy	*At a Lunar Eclipse*
Gerard Manley Hopkins	*Starlight Night*

Mystery

Thomas D'Urfey	*I'll Sail upon the Dog Star*
Ted Hughes	*The Earth, the Owl and other Moon People* (23 moon poems)
Judith Wright	*Full Moon Rhyme*

Narrative

Robert Graves	*Star Talk*
James Kirkup	*Tea in a Space Ship*

Prose Extracts

The Bible	Genesis – Chapter One
H. G. Wells	*The Time Machine*

News reports which feature current space programmes of the U.S.A. and U.S.S.R.

God and Heaven

God and Heaven

Religious Education may appear at first glance to be outside the scope of this book. A themative approach to God and Heaven seems patronising to say the least! Yet in reality it is often difficult to separate the spiritual from the temporal. Is this really surprising? The 1959 *Handbook of Suggestions for Teachers in Primary Schools* (HMSO) states 'Much of what is often described as history might equally well pass for English, Religious Instruction, Art, Craft or Geography . . . Religious Instruction should link up with other subjects. Is Wilberforce or Shaftesbury or St. Francis a figure in religious instruction or in history or in both? Is the 23rd Psalm English or Scripture or both?'

Thus I would suggest that the possible sources of inspiration for creative work are many and would stress that modern techniques are as appropriate for religious instruction as in the more secular parts of the curriculum. 'A scheme should consider the means which are necessary to serve the end in view. Pictures, maps, books, film strips, the place of puppetry, painting and modelling – all these need as much attention in the scheme of religious education as in other subjects' (1959 *Handbook*). In passing I should make the point that the Plowden report does put a great question mark over this ideal of linking RI with all the other subjects. 'Can an integral curriculum include religious education when individual parents may not wish their children to receive it and certain teachers may not feel competent or wish to give it?'

So much by way of general introduction. I merely wish to establish the fact that RI should not be seen as a subject immersed in antiquity which deserves nothing more than the most formal treatment and is utterly divorced from the rest of the curriculum and from Life (which surely is what religious education should be about).

The obvious starting point for material from which the theme can grow is the Bible. The stories may be used simply for picture-making or for free writing and movement as well. The list which follows is not meant to be exhaustive, but it does indicate the range available. Plowden suggests that too much emphasis is still being placed on the Old Testament element in scriptural teaching and the following list certainly errs in this respect. It is, however, deliberate, since there is more Old Testament material which lends itself to dramatic presentation in movement and in the visual arts.

Old Testament

The Creation	Solomon's Temple – its building
Noah's Ark	Belshazzar's Feast
Joseph	The Lion's Den
Moses and the Burning Bush	Shadrach, Meshach and Abednego
The Golden Calf	Jehu's Chariot
David and the Bear	Jonah and the Whale

The attack on Jericho	Jacob's Ladder

New Testament

The Nativity	Healing miracles
The child Jesus in the Temple	Good Friday and Easter
Storm on Lake Galilee	The adventures of Paul
Clearing the Temple	The New Jerusalem and the beasts
Flight into Egypt	of St. John's vision (Revelation)

There is much recorded music which will link with these stories. The extracts should be kept short and chosen with care so that the maximum dramatic effect is achieved.

But surely the purpose of religious instruction is to show how the broad principles of life which the Bible contains may be applied to the lives of ordinary men and women. This might be attempted through literature (*Pilgrim's Progress, The Canterbury Tales, The Little Flowers of St. Francis,* Bede's *Ecclesiastical History*). Another approach is through the lives of contemporary men and women (eg. Schweitzer, Father Damian) and through the lives of local saints (eg. Felix and Fursey, Boniface, Alciun, Paulinus, Cuthbert, Chad, Alban, Hugh of Lincoln, Margaret of Scotland).

Historical events linked with visits to local places of interest will also help children realise that Christian belief spans the centuries and that people have been prepared to work, give and even suffer for their faith. There is, for example, an excellent diorama in Norwich Museum showing St. Edmund's last battle with the Danes. At St. Bartholomew's, Smithfield, in London, it is easy to recapture something of the spirit of Rahere, Richard I's jester who founded a hospital (legend has it) in return for his recovery from a dangerous illness. On a less romantic note we have the great wooden winch in the roof of Peterborough Cathedral – which was used 800 years ago to pull up stones for the building of the church.

A group of children I took to see it expressed some amazement that people could have 'worked that high up, building, with no proper tools – just for a church!' The wool churches (eg. Lavenham), the ruins of great monasteries, local charities which are still administered (eg, Castle Rising almshouses), the statues of local men and women which dot our village streets and town squares – all can be used as the starting points for discussion and research. Why did Edith Cavell die? Why was patriotism not enough? (A child's question on passing her statue by the National Portrait Gallery.) Did Wilberforce really care about slaves? What made Robert Owen try to create a new society around his mill in Lanarkshire? Did Chamberlain really help Birmingham's poor? The children's discoveries, when they follow research along these lines, recorded in notes, models and drawings may not all point to idealism prompted by Christian belief, but they will provide the child with some tangible examples on which he can build.

The London agreed syllabus puts this point very succinctly; 'The great fact to be established in the minds of the children is that Christian men and women have witnessed continually since Christianity began, have lived in all sorts of conditions and express themselves in many and varied ways.' Plowden suggests that examples selected should embrace the Christian and the non Christian . . . 'that Saladin, for example, is as relevant as St. Bernard.' If we accept this the range of things we can paint and model (within the broad sweep of RI) is extended considerably.

So much for theory. Let me conclude with some practical suggestions for art and craft work, bearing in mind that many of them could be used as visual material for the school assembly, whether it be taken by the children or by a member of the staff.

1. Take the children on expeditions to churches and cathedrals. Try to arrange for a guide who should be asked to emphasise the people who have been associated with the place rather than the glories of the building. (Does a Norman Triforium interest a child as much, for example, as the man in Wimbourne who wanted to be buried half in the church and half outside it, half above the ground and half below it – and was?) Give the group ample time to make large scale sketches of the building, outside as well as in, of monuments and plaques. If there are brasses obtain permission for rubbings to be taken – not by the whole class, one copy is surely sufficient for a display. For rubbings you will require detail paper; drawings should be on heavy-weight sugar paper. Use Finart/Freart range for both activities.

2. Take the children to museums. There are a number which are devoted to national leaders, and men of letters (eg. Wesley's House in Old Street, London) and to people who have been inspired to right wrongs (eg. Thomas Coram's Hospital for Foundling children). Index Publishers, 27/28, Finsbury Square, London E.C.2 produce a handbook which gives details of all museums and art galleries in the United Kingdom, opening times, cost, party rates, etc. It is published annually in January and may be obtained from most large newsagents and stationers.

3. Use the visit work for classroom and library exhibitions or for material for assemblies so that the whole school can benefit. This could embrace such things as medicine, great lives, places we have visited (eg. Canterbury, York, Walsingham, Westminster Abbey, St. Giles Cathedral).

4. Model-making and picture-making linked with the church's year. This is the approach most commonly used and there is little point in expanding it here.

The Hadow Report (1931) stated 'Religious teaching cannot be confined within the limits of any syllabus.' The point I wish to emphasise is that we should not exclude it from the thematic approach to learning which I am advocating because it is somehow 'different' from other subjects in the curriculum.

Music

Composer	Title of work
J. S. Bach	*Christmas Oratorio*
	St John Passion
	St Matthew Passion
Berlioz	*The Childhood of Christ*
Britten	*Noye's Fludde*
	The Fiery Furnace
Elgar	*The Apostles*
	The Dream of Gerontius
Handel	*Israel in Egypt*
	Messiah
	Saul
	Solomon
	'Arrival of the Queen of Sheba'
Haydn	*The Creation*
Honegger	*King David*
Mendelssohn	*Elijah*
Saint-Saëns	*Samson and Delilah*
Walton	*Belshazzar's Feast*

Other music suitable for incidental teaching and quiet listening before, during and after Assemblies, includes:

Allegri	The *Miserere*
Stanford	*Magnificat* in G
Mozart	'The Kyrie' from *Spatzenmesse*, K.220
	Exsultate Jubilate
Verdi	Extracts from *The Requiem Mass*

Poetry

Descriptive
Emily Dickinson	*A Day*
Siegfried Sassoon	*Morning Glory*
Shelley	*To Jane – the Invitation*
Henry Treece	*Christ Child*

Historical
Anon	*Little David*
Charles Causley	*Innocents' Song*
James Kirkup	*Eve of Christmas*
Christina Rossetti	*Christmas Daybreak*
J. Short	*There was a Boy Bedden in Bracke*|
Robert Southwell	*Bethlehem*
Andrew Young	*Christmas Day*

Humorous
Wilfred Owen	*Parable of the Old Men*
Louis Macniece	*Sunday Morning*

Lyrical
Anon	*Matthew, Mark, Luke and John*
Blake	*Auguries of Innocence* (extracts)
G. K. Chesterton	*Children's song*
George Herbert	*Easter*
Gerard Manley Hopkins	*Pied Beauty*
Fiona Macleod	*Kye Song of St Bride*

Mystery
Walter de la Mare	*The Three Beggars*
T. S. Eliot	*Four Quartets*
Eleanor Farjeon	*St John's Wood*

Narrative

Anon	*A Carol for St Stephen's Day*
Hilaire Belloc	*The Birds*
T. S. Eliot	*Journey of the Magi*
Thom Gunn	*St Martin*
Milton	Extracts from *Hymn on the Morning of Christ's Nativity*
Steven Ponchon	*Shepherds' Tale*

Prose

Bede	*A History of the English Church and People*, translated by Leo Sherley Price, (Penguin)
The Bible	Genesis Chapter 8 v 22, Chapter 9 v 12
Kenneth Grahame	'God Pan' (from *The Wind in the Willows*)

Ice and Snow

Ice and Snow

'January brings the snow, makes our feet and fingers glow.' So runs the old rhyme. Snowfall offers tremendous scope for writing and picture-making. Yet how rarely is it seized upon with enthusiasm, being more often regarded merely as a useful addition to the list of possible painting subjects than as a theme which allows for a great variety of creative work. Snow interests children. One could begin by trying to catch a single snow flake on a sheet of perspex (or plate glass) and study it through a magnifying glass. Budding mathematicians in the group will notice that all snow flakes have six sides or angles. However intricate the internal pattern of the ice crystals, the flake will always be hexagonal. Pattern work follows naturally upon this discovery – snowflake shapes being drawn from memory, or, better still, quick sketches made immediately after studying a flake through the magnifying glass or pocket microscope. These patterns may be painted or cut from cartridge or pastel paper. However they are made this is a useful exercise in symmetry. For maximum effect display the flakes on a sheet of black or dark blue sugar paper.

Younger children (for whom the process described above would prove too difficult) can make snow flakes from paper table doilies. Again they need to be cut into six-sided symmetrical figures. To give the flakes strength coat them with gold or silver metallic paint. They may then be displayed flat, or, if both sides have been painted, used for a mobile. Hang a hoop from the ceiling – but not from a light fitting – and tie the painted flakes to it, using fine white cotton or thread.

Picture-making using snow as a theme may be approached in a variety of ways. If paint is to be used it is best to restrict the palette. Thus older children might be reasonably expected to work the bulk of their picture in white, black and blue, mixing these three colours to give tonal contrast. Younger children should not, of course, be confined in this way although it might be salutary for them to look at snow on rooftops and hillsides before they attempt to paint a similar winter scene for themselves. One or two of the more perceptive children might notice that sunlight adds a subtle touch of blue to the overall whiteness of the landscape.

Effective snow pictures can also be produced with white pastel or chalk and charcoal on blue sugar paper. Tonal contrast is achieved by mixing the chalks with the finger tips. A red pastel (or chalk) will also be required if people appear prominently in the picture to add warmth to faces, hands and knees. Pastel pictures will require fixing before storage. The fixative is applied by mouth diffuser. (These cost a few pence each and are obtainable from most art shops or direct from any of the leading artists' colourmen). Young children (older infants, lower juniors) may find it easier to adopt a simple silhouette approach for their snow pictures. The background is prepared first. This is best textured by applying a thick coat of paint with a lino roller or a sponge. When dry silhouettes of houses, people, trees, animals and vehicles are drawn onto this in black or brown paint or indian ink. A dab of white paint here and there will give a wintry character to the whole picture.

If the children have been using snow as a theme for painting and if this has flowed naturally from playing in snow it is quite likely that some descriptive writing will be forthcoming. 'Games in the snow' is an obvious starting point (although perhaps rather commonplace). Children of ability might prefer to attempt to describe a snow flake or a walk through snowy woods or streets. The peculiar effect that snow has on sounds will need to be brought to the attention of all but the most gifted members of the group. It is helpful to suggest that successful writing often draws on all the senses – sight, touch, taste and smell, as well as hearing. One eight-year-old with whom I did some work of the type described above remarked that she could not taste snow but 'the feel of the cold round it bit into my throat' – an interesting comparison this with the poet Laurie Lee's 'when we breathed the air it smelt like needles and stabbed our nostrils'.

Models of snow scenes do not appeal to me personally, although I saw some excellent snowmen made from cotton wool and jam jars by a ten-year-old who got the idea from a 'Blue Peter' TV programme. Occasionally, however, models are required for environmental study projects. Expanded polystyrene (available from ironmongers in the form of ceiling tiles) is the cheapest method of snow landscaping. The tiles are simply broken into tiny pieces which are then piled into realistic snow drifts. Remember that not all adhesives are suitable for use with polystyrene. PVA and Marvin will stick the scraps together most successfully.

The theme can be further extended by reading poetry and prose and by playing a number of 'musical sound pictures'.

History also provides rich sources on which to draw. These could range from modern trans-polar expeditions to Scott's last journey, the debacle of Napoleon's retreat from Moscow in 1812 and the famous Great Frost on the Thames. One might end with this entry from the diary of Jonathan Swift.

'It has snowed terribly all night and is vengeance cold. 'Tis a good proverb the Devonshire people have:

> Walk fast in snow
> In frost walk slow
> And still as you go
> Tread on your toe
> When frost and snow are both together
> Sit by the fire and spare shoe leather'.

London. 21 January 1711

Music

Composer	Title of work
Bax	*Winter Legends*
Borodin	*In the Steppes of Central Asia*
Debussy	*Children's Corner*, No. 4 'Snow is dancing'
Haydn	From *The Seasons*: Introduction to 'Spring' Prelude to 'Winter'
Mahler	Slow movement from *Symphony No. 9*
Meyerbeer	*Les Patineurs*
Mozart (L)	'Musical sleigh ride'
Prokofiev	'Sleigh Ride' from *Lieutenant Kije*
Tchaikovsky	'The Months' – *Troika en Traineaux*
Vaughan Williams	*Symphony No. 7, Antarctica* – extracts
Vivaldi	*The Seasons*
Waldteufel	*Skater's Waltz*

Poetry

Descriptive

Edmund Blunden	*Midnight Skaters*
Robert Bridges	*London Snow*
Cane	*Snow Towards Evening*
Walter de la Mare	*Winter*
	The Snowman
Robert Frost	*Stopping by Woods on a Snowy Evening*
Thomas Hardy	*Snow in the Suburbs*
Keats	Opening of *The Eve of St Agnes*
Longfellow	*Excelsior*
Shakespeare	'When icicles hang by the wall' – *Love's Labour's Lost*
Wordsworth	'Skating' from *The Prelude*: 'So through the darkness and the cold we flew'

Lyrical

Walter de la Mare	*Snowflake*
Keats	*A Drear Nighted December*
Shakespeare	'Blow, blow thou winter wind' – *As You Like It*
James Thomson	*To a Snowflake*
Walt Whitman	*To a Locomotive in Winter*
Andrew Young	*Last Snow*

Mystery

Wordsworth	*Lucy Gray*

Narrative

Edmund Blunden	*Winter in East Anglia*
Walter de la Mare	*The Snow*
Robert Graves	*A Frosty Night*
Alun Lewis	*Midwinter*
Edward Thomas	*Snow*

Prose

The Sea

FR.95

The Sea

We are an island people. It is not surprising, therefore, that the sea is very much part of our lives. Even if we live in the great urban centres of London, Birmingham or Manchester the sea is still comparatively near. For centuries we have been dependent upon our navies, and ships and seamen have played a vital part in our development as a nation.

Since I began teaching I have only met one boy who had no conception of the sea and its power. Standing on the cliffs near Swanage he asked me 'Is this sea the same as the sea at Southend? I saw it there when I was little'. On being told that it was possible to sail from Swanage to Southend – and thence to America and Australia if need be – he remarked 'Coo, its all round us, like the sky.' Most English children, however, have what poets describe as 'the sea in their blood'. What else should we expect from a people well schooled in the art of seamanship, ready to man ships in the ever expanding quest for trade routes, ever ready to defend them in time of war?

Creative work in writing, movement, painting and model-making is easiest to stimulate when all the children in the group have some basic experience on which to draw. Thus the sea provides a useful starting point. The majority of the class will, at some time or another, have splashed and paddled, built sand castles, scrambled over rocks and played in pools left by the ebbing tide. While it is sometimes necessary to read a poem, play a record or look at a picture to provoke discussion, the seaside usually evokes tremendous interest without any preparatory activity whatsoever. I often use a sea topic for creative work immediately after a holiday when many of the group will have spent at least one day on the coast. With older children (10 and 11 year olds) I use the experience as a starting point for discussion. What does the sea taste like? What does it smell like? How would you describe the feeling of stones and sand on your feet, between your toes? What colours are there in the sea at daytime when the sky is overcast, in bright sunlight, at evening when the sun is setting, when the lights are on along the front? Describe the sounds of the sea – over rocks, over sand, over pebbles.

These first attempts at recapturing the sea in its various moods could be supported by sea pictures (either photographs or reproductions of famous pictures by such artists as Turner, Courbet, Seurat, Dufy, Cézanne, Desnoyer, Sisley, Monet). With younger children these pictures (or the music and poetry listed below) would provide an excellent starting point and a natural lead into discussion along the lines already mentioned. The first written work that the children attempt might simply be lists of adjectives or short descriptions of the particular qualities of the sea. Some children will almost immediately record their experiences or impressions in blank verse; others will tend to keep to straightforward prose (which, strangely enough most children find much harder to manage because of the greater discipline required).

Music will give the group a pattern of sea sounds which will help explore the subject at greater depth. My appreciation of Mendelssohn's 'The Hebrides' has been somewhat marred by an over-enthusiastic music teacher who maintained that the work was based on a 'rhythmic song' – the words of which were 'How blue the sea is, how blue the sea is'. However 'The Hebrides' should not be ignored on these very personal grounds, provided future generations of children are not subjected to similar treatment.

There is a great store of suitable music. Occasionally the story (often to be found on the record sleeves) can be told between excerpts of the music. This may provoke writing and painting – retelling the story as if the child were the storyteller or personally involved as a character in the story. Thus bright ten and eleven-year-olds might write an imaginary diary of the 'Flying Dutchman' or describe a journey on the strange waters which surround the castle of Tuonela. Even if no writing is attempted there is sufficient variety in the music listed below to evoke the different moods of the sea; this is extremely important if part of the movement lesson is to be given over to further exploration of the topic.

With such a wide range of stimuli available to arouse and sustain interest the art and craft work which grows with it should be extremely varied. The type of activity which the children will attempt will to some extent be determined by the way the teacher has allowed the topic to evolve. Thus if an historical approach has been followed models of famous ships (*Golden Hind, Revenge, Santa Maria*) might be the most popular project. Similarly a study of food supply and trade routes might result in map making, models, and pictures of dockside scenes; if however, the sea has been treated as a place of mystery and magic large murals of underwater palaces, sea nymphs, mermen and exotic fish might result.

10. A Georgian theme developed through pictures (90″ × 45″). Group work (nine and ten year olds).

69

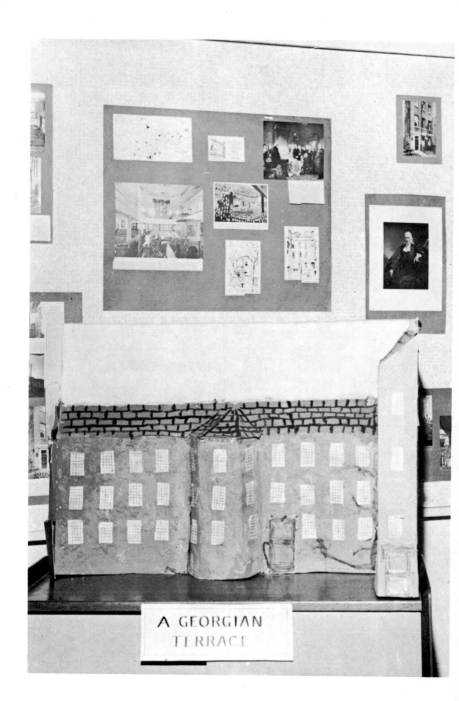

11. . . . cardboard models (nine year old).

12. . . . and group displays (nine and ten year olds).

Music

Composer	Title of work
Anon	Folk song *Blow the Wind Southerly*
Beethoven	*Pastoral Symphony* (No. 6) 4th movement, 'The Storm'
Berlioz	Overture, *Le Corsaire*
Britten	'The Four Sea Pictures' (interludes) from *Peter Grimes*
Debussy	*La Mer*
Delius	'En Bateau' from *Petite Suite 1899*
Elgar	*Sea Songs*
Grieg	*The Return of Peer Gynt*, storm scene, Act V, scene 1
Mendelssohn	Overture, *The Hebrides*
	Overture, *Calm Sea and Prosperous Voyage*
Respighi	*Fountains of Rome*
Rimsky-Korsakov	*Scheherazade*, 1st and 4th movements
Saint-Saëns	From *Carnival of Animals:* *The Aquarium* *The Swan*
Schubert	*The Trout*
Smetana	*Má Vlast*
C. V. Stanford	*Songs of the Sea* *Songs of the Fleet*
Wagner	Overture to *The Flying Dutchman*

Sea shanties – both recordings and ones which children can learn.

Poetry

Descriptive

W. H. Auden	*Seascape*
A. Cunningham	*A Wet Sheet*
Robert Frost	*Sand Dunes*
	Once by the Pacific
Zulfikhar Ghose	*Coming to England*
Gerard Manley Hopkins	*Deutschland*
Rudyard Kipling	*The Last Chanty*
John Masefield	*Sea Fever*
Andrew Young	*Dead Crab*

Historical

Anon	*Death of Admiral Benbow*
Charles Causley	*Keats at Teignmouth*
Sir Henry Newbolt	*Drake's Drum*
Tennyson	*The Revenge*

Humorous

Anon	*Eddystone Light*
W. H. Auden	*Lobster Pot*
Hilaire Belloc	*The Whale*
W. H. Davies	*Sailor to his Parrot*
W. S. Gilbert	*We sailed d'ye see* (from *Ruddigore*)
E. V. Rieu	*The Flattered Flying Fish*
	Tony the Turtle

Lyrical

Walter de la Mare	*Echoes*
James Reeves	*The Sea*

Mystery

Clifford Dyment	*Singing Sailor*
James Elroy Flecker	*Lord Arnaldos*
Wilfrid Gibson	*Flannan Isle*
Judith Wright	*The Surfer*

Narrative

Anon	*Sir Patrick Spens*
	The Mermaid
Charles Causley	*Convoy*
Coleridge	*The Rime of the Ancient Mariner*
Jean Ingelow	*High Tide on the Coast of Lincolnshire*
Alan Ross	*Night Patrol*
Ian Serraillier	*Ballad of Kon Tiki*
Robert Southey	*The Inchcape Rock*

Prose

Anon	Beowulf's fight with the Sea Monster
The Bible	The story of Jonah
	Psalm 107 v 23-31
	Storm on the Sea of Galillee (Mark 4 v 35-41)
	The Journey of St Paul
R. M. Ballantyne	*Coral Island*
Joseph Conrad	*Typhoon*
J. Y. Cousteau	*The Silent World*
Sir Arthur Grimble	*A Pattern of Islands* (Lagoon Days)
Ernest Hemingway	*The Old Man and the Sea*
Thor Heyerdahl	*Kon Tiki*
Homer	*The Iliad* and *The Odyssey* (retold for children by J. Watson, published by Paul Hamlyn)
G. Mulhauser	*The Cruise of the Amaryllis*
A. Ross	*The Wreck of the Moni*
Joshua Slocum	*Sailing Alone Around the World*
Robert Louis Stevenson	*Treasure Island*
R. Stock	*Cruise of the Dream Ship*

See also: *Ships, Sailors and Pirates.*

SHIPS SAILORS AND PIRATES

Ships, Sailors and Pirates

Most children are fascinated by boats. When being taken round a ship like the *Discovery* or the *Victory* it is noticeable that the questions girls ask are often far more pertinent than those asked by boys; so there is little to fear when introducing this topic to a mixed class of nine and ten year olds.

I suppose most of us have, from time to time, used ships and seamen as a vehicle for the teaching of history. Colonial expansion is much more exciting if told through the adventures of Captain Cook, the Cabots or Henry the Navigator than it is through dates, trade charters or lists of imports. Indeed the names of great explorers are often linked with that of a particular ship – the *Golden Hind* and the *Terra Nova*, for example, are almost as well known as Drake and Scott, and who thinks of Nelson without the *Victory* or Chichester without *Gypsy Moth*?

The men and the ships . . . we can deal with the men reasonably adequately, using extracts from contemporary diaries to bring them alive, by displaying *Jackdaws*[1] where appropriate, by taking the children to art galleries where they can study their portraits and their dress, to museums to see pictures and dioramas illustrating their life and times.

Yet the ships present a rather different problem. One can take children aboard a few fairly modern vessels, but can we really give them any appreciation at all of a Viking longboat (other than through a picture from Unstead's *Looking at History*) or a Phoenician galley? I think we can do a little by encouraging the children to make simple models and asking them to imagine the difficulties involved in sailing it across rough uncharted seas. The boy who made the longboat (Plate 16) was only ten years old but he wrote the following when comparing his model with a paddle steamer: 'These Vikings didn't have much protection . . . and they had to row some of the way. It must have been much more comfortable in a great iron ship. Think of the waves breaking over the shields and the cold winds blowing through your cloak. They must have been clever to navigate by the stars.' Meanwhile the boy modelling the paddle steamer (Plate 15) was forced to think about the reasons for paddles being used instead of screws, of steam instead of sail, of iron instead of wood. Does not all of this necessitate thoughtful enquiry, the assimilation of knowledge almost accidentally (and knowledge so gained is rarely forgotten)?

Models as simple as the ones illustrated in Plates 15 and 16 are not difficult to make. They are based on a simple line drawing of the shape of the hull on a sheet of thin strawboard. This is then cut out and used as a template to give an exact copy for the second side. These two pieces are then taped together at the prow. If a flat end is required at the stern, as in a galleon, a card strip is taped in before this end is joined together (see diagram). By placing a cardboard box or a scrap of wood between these two

1 *Published by Jonathan Cape, 12s. per set.*

ard shapes we can push out the sides and thus give any necessary shaping) the hull. From here it is a simple matter to cover the hull with paste and aper strips to form the deck and when this is dry the superstructure can e built. If acrylic colours are available these are ideal for painting the model and will also give it additional strength. If this is not possible a mixture of powder colour and gum will do almost as well. Sails and rigging re best left until last. For sails I would suggest that cartridge paper be used s it keeps its shape well and can be gently bent into almost any position. Rigging always presents a problem, but thin thread or cotton looks realistic provided it is not too sparse. Dressmaker's pins, pushed into the decking, will hold it in place temporarily and a coat of balsa cement or PVA over the pin heads is usually sufficient to make it quite permanent.

GALLEON

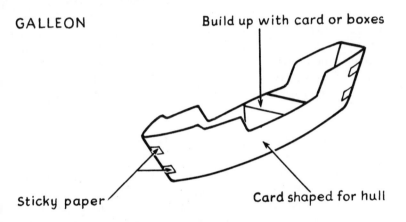

Build up with card or boxes

Sticky paper

Card shaped for hull

When a collection of ships has been made a display could be mounted with each child, or group of children, providing some written explanation of the model. It might prove necessary to mount some of the ships on bases – there could be lengths of fabric, painted or textured boards, or even sheets of plate glass or perspex.

Whenever possible the children engaged on a study of this nature should be given some opportunity of studying ships at first hand – even if this only involves a trip to a nearby canal or river. Recently the children with whom I have been working have been on a fire float, a police launch, a tug, a lifeboat, toured a working dockyard and visited the *Cutty Sark* and the *Discovery*. The reactions were many and varied. One girl asked, 'Why are ships always Hers, Sir?' While searching for an answer a boy replied, 'My Dad says everything of value is Hers – perhaps that's got something to do with it.' I left it at that!

Let us turn now to the men who used the ships. I have already suggested that the great voyages of discovery are a useful starting point – but they are perhaps so familiar to teachers that the excitement tends to be lost through repetition. But however often smuggling and pirate stories are told the magic remains, somehow typified in this verse remembered from childhood (and no doubt still to be found in most school anthologies):

> 'I've asked a great many people
> But nobody seems to know
> How the pirates kept their Christmas
> In the days of long ago.'

For me this illustrates the fact that over the years these sea robbers have come to occupy a unique place in the imaginative life of the young child. Why should this be? Living on the Barbary coast must indeed have been barbaric, although some semblance of order was maintained during the reign of the first Pasha of Algiers, Khair-ed-Din Barbarossa. There are few captains who have been remembered by posterity in the same light as Robin Hood, although one exception is Bartholomew Roberts who is said to have been brave, kind and generous and whose death off the coast of Africa (1720) in a sea battle was felt to be rather premature, even for a pirate.

What of the rest? The life of Sir Henry Morgan (1630-88) will interest children for it indicates that piracy was a useful political weapon and was not only taken up as a career by those crossed in love or ill-used in law. Sir Henry was a pirate whose work was blessed by government backing; so much so that he ended up as Lieutenant-Governor of Jamaica. Children will find his life full of excitement, particularly the attacks he lead on Puerto Bello and Panama, where, legend has it, the Spanish foot-soldiers were supported by herds of wild bulls.

William Dampier (1652-1715) is another 'real life' pirate of whom something is known. He was a writer, a slave trader (he brought back an Indian prince from one voyage and sold him to raise capital), a naval captain (until he was court martialled) and in the latter part of his life a successful pirate, returning from the South Seas with booty well in excess of £150,000. He died before he could spend it. Then there is Captain Kidd (1652-1701) whose life of violence ended, like that of many another pirate, in chains at Execution Dock, Wapping.

From historical pirates one can turn to fictional ones. Captain Hook (from *Peter Pan*) always filled me with terror as a child, (even though he was eaten by a ticking crocodile). Somehow he is more sinister on the stage than ever Long John Silver was in print or in film. Poetry also has much to offer (see below).

Discussion around pirates and piracy might well lead to work on smugglers and revenue men. One of the most exciting stories for ten to twelve-year-olds is *Moonfleet* (Penguin) which has everything from ghostly coffins, a long chase, treasure, a little bloodshed, requited love and a happy ending. It is certainly 'a must' for all children who live along the South Coast, for much of the action takes place in Dorset. Turning to poetry again, we have Rudyard Kipling's *A Smuggler's Song* . . . . 'If you wake at midnight and hear a horse's feet . . .' James Reeve's *Rum Lane* and the old ballad *The Smuggler* which begins 'O my true love's a smuggler and sails on the sea'.

So much for sources of information. How can it best be used? I have deliberately linked this theme to 'Ships'. While not wishing to concentrate on the less wholesome side of the life of a sailor, both smugglers and pirates can be used to breathe an air of magic, mystery and romance into the dry bones of men o' war and the press gang. The poems listed will certainly trigger off writing. I have included de la Mare's *The Picture* because so many questions are left unanswered. The sailor comes to the inn at twilight, carrying a bundle – why? Where has he come from? What does he want? Who is he seeking? Shades here of black spot in *Treasure Island*. I have found that children write on this topic freely and with feeling.

'The sea breeze played in my hair. I sensed danger. The moon shone down on the pebbly beach. We sat there, waiting: my heart beating, the sweat running down my face although it was bitterly cold. Suddenly a shadow out to sea. The call! The cry of a gull . . . .

We carefully took the barrels from the boat fearing every minute that the coastguards would come. Then to the cave . . . our job was done.'

(Christine, aged ten)

The subject also offers tremendous scope for lively picture-making. This could range from pirate masks made from card to fabric collage and appliqué.

Music

Composer	Title of work
Beethoven	Dervish chorus from *Ruins of Athens*
Walton	Overture, *Portsmouth Point*

See: sea music, page 64, all of which is suitable.

Poetry

PIRATES AND SMUGGLERS

Descriptive

Anon	*The Smuggler*
Vincent Benêt	*Captain Kidd*
Walter de la Mare	*The Picture*
	The Old Sailor
Clifford Dyment	*Singing Sailor*
Mary Gilmore	*Old Botany Bay*
John Masefield	*A Ballad of John Silver*
James Reeves	*Rum Lane*

Historical

John Masefield	*Captain Stratton's fancy*

Humorous

Matilda Meigs	*Pirate Don Dirk*
E. V. Rieu	*Pirates on Funafuti*
Robert Louis Stevenson	*Pirate Story*

Lyrical

Anon	*O My True Love's a Smuggler*
Walter de la Mare	*Araby*
Lady Anne Lindsay	*Spanish Gold*

Mystery

E. V. Rieu	*Pirate Passes*

Narrative

Anon	*Henry Martyn*
Charles Kingsley	*The Last Buccaneer*
Rudyard Kipling	*Smuggler's Song*
John Masefield	*Spanish Waters*
Robert Southey	*The Inchcape Rock*
Sir John Squire	*Landing at Night*

Poetry

SHIPS

Descriptive

Anglo Saxon	*The Seafarer* (Beowulf's voyage to Denmark v 194-257)
James Elroy Flecker	*The Old Ships*
Wilfred Gibson	*The Wreck*
Arthur Waley	*Boating in Autumn*
Walt Whitman	*Dismantled Ship*

Historical

Cowper	*Loss of the Royal George*
Robert Graves	*Nelson's Funeral*
Thomas Hardy	*Night of Trafalgar*
Sir Henry Newbolt	*The Old Superb*
Macaulay	*The Armada*
Tennyson	*The Revenge*

Humorous

Edward Lear	*The Jumblies*
	The Owl and the Pussy Cat
	The Old Man in a Barge
M. Thwaites	*The Jevis Bay*

Lyrical

E. Anderson	*The Clipper* Dunbar *to the Clipper* Cutty Sark
Rudyard Kipling	*Big Steamers*
John Masefield	*Cargoes*

Mystery

Charles Causley	*Nursery Rhyme of Innocence and Experience*
Cicely Fox-Smith	*Ghosts in Deptford*
Shakespeare	'Clarence's Dream' (*Richard III* Act I, scene 4)

Poetry

Narrative

Prose

PIRATES AND SMUGGLERS

J. M. Barrie	*Peter Pan*
Daphne du Maurier	*Jamaica Inn*
J. Connell	*Return of Long John Silver*
J. M. Falkner	*Moonfleet*
John Masefield	*Jim Davies*
S. Meader	*Black Buccaneer*
P. Rush	*He Went with Dampier*
A. Seligman	*Thunder Reef*
Robert Louis Stevenson	*Treasure Island*
Russell Thorndike	*Doctor Syn*

SHIPS

The Bible	Psalm 107
R. H. Dana	*Two Years Before The Mast*
Alain Gerbault	*The Fight of the Fire Crest*
	In Quest of the Sun
Charles Kingsley	*Westward Ho!*
Pierre Loti	*Iceland Fisherman*
W. Mantyr	*Southsea Man*
Herman Melville	*Moby Dick*

MASKS MAPS NATIVES

Masks, Maps and Natives

From time to time most of us must have been involved in a mask project with a group of children. Possibly the interest has been aroused by a book on primitive cultures or as a result of a visit to a museum, such as Horniman or the Commonwealth Institute. More often than not, however, the starting point is in drama and from discussion of folk customs (such as Hallowe'en or Guy Fawkes). Masks fascinate because they are primitive and in an children are primitives too. An interesting parallel may be drawn between children's art and the art of primitive societies, religions and civilisations.

Making masks provides tremendous scope for pattern work and herein lie its great value. Too often, pattern-making becomes a rather purposeless activity unrelated to either painting, model-making or fabric decoration.

The simplest way of producing a perfectly balanced mask is to work on lightweight white paper. Fold the paper vertically down the centre. One half of the mask is drawn in outline on this sheet in black wax crayon – one half of the nose running down the centre fold. When this has been completed hold the paper, still folded, against a window. The design will show through. By using this as a guide it is a simple process to make an exact copy by over drawing in crayon while the paper is still against the window. Open the fold and colour the mask in wax crayon or paint.

If a more substantial mask is required (for drama or for dimensional display) cut out the paper shape and mount it on card after colouring. Interesting effects can be obtained by colouring the whole mask in heavy layers of crayon. The paper is then crumbled so that the wax cracks. Smooth out the paper and apply a wash of ebony stain or ink over the whole mask with brush or small sponge. The stain will run into the cracks caused when the waxed paper was folded and give an attractive crazing to the whole design.

Large masks are best made from card. Boxes give an excellent base and features are simple to build up from junk material such as egg cartons, packing tubes and match boxes. Eyes sometimes present a problem but by cutting a table tennis ball in half and mounting it in the eye sockets a rather terrifying appearance is quickly achieved.

Masks made from junk or boxes will need to be covered with several layers of paste and paper scraps to give a satisfactory painting surface. If possible paint the mask with acrylic colours. This will give strength to the model as well as concealing all the newsprint. If acrylics are not available use thick pre-mix powder colour or poster paint and varnish when dry.

An interest in mask-making will often lead to a search for less conventional materials. Soft brick or breeze block could be carved using a cold chisel and a light-weight hammer. New Clay[1] is also valuable in this connection because this material does not crumble. Moreover as there is very little shrinkage, models made in it do not crack as they dry. Masks made in

[1] Available from Overston House, Sunnyfield Road, Orpington, Kent.

86

New Clay may be hardened by brushing with a liquid hardener. They do not require firing and can be painted with any water or oil-based colour. Girls may like to make mask designs in fabric. The Kon Tiki (Plate 8) is a good example of what might be attempted. The design was drawn on a length of rayon in chalk and then painted with acrylic paint. These colours do not need any special priming and are light and water-fast when dry. When the design has been completed and the paint has hardened simple stitches may be used to complete the mask. This method of working can be used for all types of banners and looks particularly attractive if worked on a large scale and suspended from the ceiling of classroom, library or hall.

Mask-making might well lead into a study of the lives of primitive peoples (such as the Polynesians) and certainly there are enough suitable prose extracts which record exotic adventures on strange shores with 'wild natives'. Some of these are fact (like Captain Cook in Australia) but some of the fictional ones contain an element of truth. In this connection it is worth recording the story of Alexander Selkirk. On 1st February 1709 Alexander Selkirk was rescued by a British ship from Juan Fernandez, an island off the coast of Chile. He had spent 4 years 4 months on the island – a rather harsh penalty for quarrelling with the captain of his ship. Although Captain Rogers, the master of the ship which rescued Selkirk, wrote an account of his adventures and of his first meeting with 'a man clothed in goat skins who looked wilder than the first owners of them', it was Daniel Defoe who saw in Selkirk's adventure the possibility of a novel. So it was that *Robinson Crusoe* was created.

A story like that of Selkirk (or Crusoe) will obviously be of tremendous interest to children. The possible art and craft links are many. It might be as well to begin with the construction of an imaginary map. This might be painted on a large sheet of sugar paper or built up in papiermâché on a sheet of hardboard (or an old blackboard). With young children it is as well to encourage the use of pictures rather than symbols to mark places of interest. This will also give an opportunity to children who enjoy drawing on a small scale to come into their own. Trees, cliffs, rivers, the castaways' camp could be shown in this way. Most of the group will have some appreciation of 'picture maps' from holiday brochures and children's story books. Many editions of 'Winnie the Pooh' for example have a picture map on the flyleaf.

Having constructed the map a whole host of possibilities for model making, painting and writing present themselves. Adventures on the island, a day-by-day diary of the shipwrecked sailor (each day being written by a different child), models of his house (constructed from junk), and the ship in which he hopes to return to civilisation can be made and displayed around the map.

Robinson Crusoe is but one of a number of stories based on islands. *Coral Island* and *Treasure Island* immediately suggest themselves, although I found that the more fantastic qualities of *Gulliver* lent themselves more successfully to model- and picture-making.

Interest in fictional islands might well result in some of the group becoming interested in islands which actually exist – such as Easter Island, Iona or Lindisfarne. If the school is situated on the Isle of Wight, the Isle of Man, or the Orkneys or Shetlands there is no need to go so far afield for inspiration! Sir Arthur Grimble's *A Pattern of Islands*, which tells of life on a protectorate in the Pacific, may also be used to add an exotic quality to the study.

If a theme of this type is being developed (whether by the whole school, several classes or a small group of children from one class) part of the role of the teachers concerned will be to make sure that the work – when it is finished – is presented with care. Maps, photographs and pictures from magazines could be collected to give added impact to the children's work. The teacher should also be prepared to help when the children have an idea but not the knowhow to implement it. For example the Kon Tiki raft (Plate 13) was made to be displayed against a map on a vertical display board. Having made the boat, however, the boy concerned (a nine-year-old) could not manage to mount it.

It is at times such as this that the teacher can intervene with profit and show the children that he really cares about their creative work and will go to almost any lengths to ensure that it is seen at its best.

Music

Composer	Title of work
Arne	Incidental music to *The Tempest*
Bizet	'Habeñera' from *Carmen*
Coates	*Eastwards*
	Sleepy Lagoon
Falla	'Ritual Fire Dance' from *El Amor Brujo*
Mussorgsky	'Dance of the Persian Slaves' from *Khovantschina*, Act 4
Ravel	*Bolero*

Also : Calypso and Steel Band music from the West Indies.

Poetry

Descriptive

Roy Campbell	*The Zulu Girl*
R. Ingamells	*Black Children*
Marlowe	*Tamburlaine*, Dying Speech
A. A. Milne	*The Old Sailor*
	The Island
Sir John Squire	*The Indian*

Historical

Michael Drayton	*To the Virginian Voyage*
Sir John Squire	*There was a Native*

Humorous

W. S. Gilbert	*The Yarn of the Nancy Bell*

Lyrical

W. H. Auden	*Look, Stranger on this Island Now*
Shakespeare	*Richard II*, Gaunt's speech: 'This royal throne of kings . . . '
	Pericles, Storm scene
W. B. Yeats	*Lake Isle of Innisfree*

Mystery

Walter de la Mare	*Isle of Lone*
Cecil Day Lewis	*Wearing Again the Legendary Isle*
James Elroy Flecker	*A Ship, an Isle, a Sickle Moon*

Narrative

Blake	*The Little Black Boy*
Stephen Spender	*A Stop Watch and an Ordnance Map*
W. Watson	*Ballad of Summerwater*

Prose

Arabian Nights	'Sinbad the Sailor'
R. M. Ballantyne	*Coral Island*
Daniel Defoe	*Robinson Crusoe*
R. Gibbings	*Coconut Island*
Sir Arthur Grimble	*A Pattern of Islands*
R. Hakluyt	Voyages
Alan Ross	*Danger on Glass Island*
H. M. Stanley	*How I Found Livingstone*
Robert Louis Stevenson	*Treasure Island*
Jonathan Swift	*Gulliver's Travels*
Mark Twain	*Tom Sawyer*
J. Wyss	*The Swiss Family Robinson*

PEOPLE LONG AGO

People Long Ago

'Human curiosity is always whetted by the details of other people's lives. This is especially true when the people involved are remote in time and circumstance'[1] In a fascinating chapter of this book, 'The running of a noble household', we are shown in detail the day-to-day organisation that was required to keep the inhabitants of a castle the size of Kenilworth or Odiham functioning smoothly. The amount of grain, wine and fish that was consumed in one day reached quite frightening proportions – 400 herrings at Kenilworth on 23 February 1265. This chapter paints a dramatic picture of life in England 700 years ago and teachers who wish to use a study of the past as a starting point for creative work would do well to read it.

Children are interested in people rather than events. Samuel Pepys' diary provides a first hand description of the fire of London and the children will remember the cheese he buried rather than the number of houses destroyed or people made homeless. Recount the final days in the life of Richard III and they will recall the prophesy of the old women on the bridge over the River Soar rather than the significance of white and red roses. And this is natural, for without people what would History be?

The only way of bringing History to life and making geography meaningful is to use the children's immediate environment as a starting point. But how can one do this if the school is situated in a new town or in an industrial backwater whose roots go back only as far as the latter part of the nineteenth century? Even if this is the case, there will always be an old house, a historic church, a museum, a ruined castle or abbey not far away. Herein lies one of the joys of teaching in the British Isles.

Where is it most profitable to start? There are two possible places – churches and art galleries. Neither of these may appear as exciting as castles and museums but both may be used to recreate the lives of people.

When journeying up and down the country on teachers' refresher courses I often visit the parish church nearest the hall or school where I am to lecture. More often than not it is rich in ancient tombs with beautifully carved effigies of long dead local worthies or with brasses which contain a wealth of detail on clothing and costume. So often these direct links with the past are never used (or worse still, even thought about). Tombs may be sketched, notes made about their occupants, and their families traced with the help of parish registers. This research may take in other churches nearby and even lead to a study of place names.

The church itself – the stone it is built from and the way it has been fashioned – will often contain a wealth of history. One old priest I met showed a group of children where Cromwell's men shot bullets into his church door. 'Were you a Cavalier then, Sir, in hiding?' one nine-year-old asked, showing little time sense perhaps but a certain insight into the politics of the 1640s.

[1] *Simon de Montfort* by Margaret Wade Lebarge; Eyre and Spottiswoode.

94

When taking groups of children into old churches I try to present the building as a store house of information about our past. The children make drawings on large sheets of sugar paper using wax crayon or oil pastel. After a few experiences of 'drawing large what you see' (rather than what you thought you saw) surprising progress will be made. Time is a vital factor. When children are involved and interested they will want to finish their work without interruption and it is important to allow them as much time as possible to complete their drawings in the building. Most children – from the age of eight upwards – can produce extremely sensitive work. There is little need to suggest subjects, for they seem to know almost instinctively the thing they can draw best. Thus John concentrated on decorations on the surrounds of early fonts, Brendon on arches, Marion on the dresses she found on tombs and brasses, Peter on knights and heraldry, Maureen on boss designs and the stories and legends associated with them.

The richness of this sort of experience and the ways in which it can be recorded in books and on tape, inevitably leads to model-making, drama, and the production of maps and charts. This in turn may involve research in the local library and museum. Seeing, experiencing, talking, doing, recording, making – these are the bones on which a creative environment can grow.

Art galleries provide another starting point too often ignored. London children are fortunate in that the National Portrait Gallery houses a unique collection of portraits of famous people. Most towns have some sort of picture collection that is helpful in bringing the past alive. Thus, to select some examples from various parts of the country, the sort of questions to pose are these. 'Your great-great-grandmother wore clothes like these when she saw the launching of the Great Eastern. Describe them. How do they differ from those your mother wears today?' 'This is a picture of Waterloo Station during the first World War. What interests you about it?' 'Totnes Castle looked like this four hundred years ago. What parts can you recognise? Imagine you are by the gate. Describe the sounds you can hear.'

Several museums have a schools service which supplements this 'learning through personal discovery'. The Geffrye museum in Shoreditch, for example, has sets of period costume for the children to wear and they are allowed to handle some of the exhibits.

Like most educational terms, creative environment is used so freely as to mean almost all things to all teachers. The purpose of this book is to suggest that the child's environment – if it is to be truly creative – should not be restricted within the confines of the classroom. It is for us as teachers to use the cultural richness of our own neighbourhood to enliven, enlighten and vivify the children's learning.

Sometimes I use an approach suggested to me by the fictional Inspector Grant in Josephine Tey's novel *Daughter of Time*. In this book the Inspector investigates the murder of the Princes in the Tower and studies a portrait of Richard III for clues to his character[1]. Catherine, a nine-year-old,

[1] *Daughter of Time*, Josephine Tey, Penguin, pp 27-29.

13. Exploring the South Seas: group study of Kon Tiki (nine and ten year olds).

14. Shakespeare and the Globe. Group picture (60″ × 60″) supported by rubbings, childrens' writings and source pictures from magazines and books (eight year olds).

15. Boats from card: A paddle steamer (eight year old).

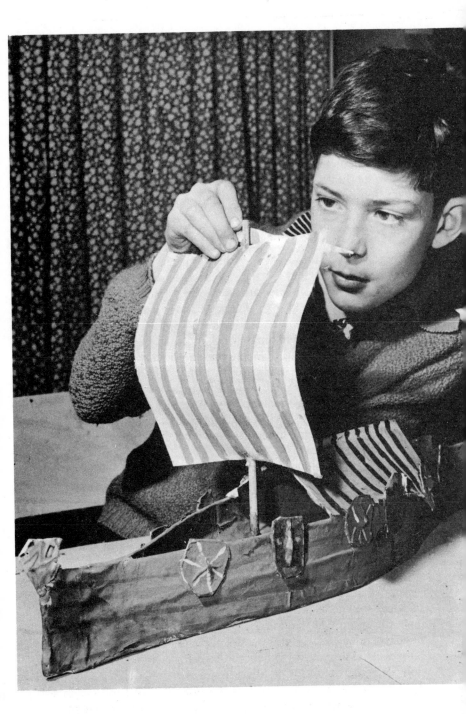

16. . . . and a Viking long ship (ten year old).

deeply involved in a study of the Highlanders of the '45 wrote this after gazing at a portrait of Charles. 'Charles Stuart stands before me, richly dressed. His skin is fair and there is a faint smile in his blue eyes. He is about eighteen years old and the son of a king. Soon he will go to Scotland to fight. I don't think I would really want to know him well. I'm not sure he could be trusted for he looks very proud.'

We have come a long way from the sort of History syllabus which reads 'Year 1 Prehistory to Romans, Year 2 Saxons to Normans, Year 3 Normans to Bosworth, Year 4 Bosworth to Elizabeth II'. There is now much greater freedom for the development of a topic which cuts across dates and historical epochs (on the sound principle that how a child learns is more important than what he learns).

Let me now illustrate how a theme can develop from quite humble beginnings into a study of considerable depth. A group of second year children had begun a local study. The early history of the area aroused little interest. There was once an abbey but few traces remained. The Tudor period, however, was rich in local associations. A street map was found in a library book showing the area in 1540. The streets were named. Were any still there today? Maps were duplicated and a group of children went off to see. Was there any evidence of buildings which stood in 1540? There was one old wall, recently uncovered, that contained an oriel window and a church in which there were some memorials to people who died in the 1500s. One person commemorated there was Fletcher, a poet. Could he have known Shakespeare? Who was Shakespeare? What did he do? How did he live? What were theatres like? What other entertainments were there? Obviously here there were so many leads that individual and group work was possible on a considerable scale.

When such a position develops the teacher needs deliberately to collect material. This should include visual aids (reproductions from contemporary sources and pictures from magazines such as *Pictorial Education*), books that have any bearing on the period (poetry, medicine, biography, art, craft, needlework, architecture, costume, hobbies, entertainments, customs) and gramophone records of appropriate music and verse.

Our Tudor theme developed along the broad lines described above. A model of the armada which had been made by a younger class was incorporated in a joint display between the two classrooms – the older children 'backing' the model with drawings of ships and sailors and their writing about the event. Old London Bridge was built from boxes, dolls dressed in Tudor costumes, a large wall picture of the Globe theatre made from paper cutouts. After listening to some recorded extracts from Henry V a number of children prepared a study on Shakespeare and his plays. Christine imagined that she was going to see a play performed by 'The Lord Chamberlain's Company'. She wrote 'I dressed quickly, took some money from my father's chest and hurried to the Globe. There were crowds of people pushing, shouting, jostling. There was a great puddle in the road and I had to pull my dress up and jump across as best I could. I paid to go in. An actor came out on the stage to announce the play. We cheered and shouted. It had begun . . .' In similar vein John wrote 'My feet are cold. People are complaining and shouting loudly. So many are muttering that I can hardly hear the actors speaking, but it must be difficult acting in the open air.' (Plate 14).

It so happened that this period of intense interest coincided with a TV series on the Tudors. The fact that it was aimed at the 11-13 age range did not prevent nine-year-olds from watching with interest and enthusiasm. The incidents on film were full of action, the children were familiar with the dress and customs. This prompts me to ask whether we always use TV and radio as wisely as we might. There is often the odd programme in a series which, when married to an existing classroom study, will give the children still more material to develop. I make this point because flexibility of time-table is essential if work of the type I am describing is to be successfully accomplished.

Musicians, poets, writers, architects, dress designers and craftsmen in wood, clay and metal – these are the people whose creative flair can still be appreciated by the present generation of school children. It is therefore to these people that we should turn in our attempts to help children understand the past and realise their own innate potential.

Let me illustrate this point by turning once again to the sixteenth century. Shakespeare dwarfs most of his contemporaries in the field of letters but children will also be interested in the works of John Skelton, Edmund Spencer, Christopher Marlow, Ben Jonson, John Donne, John Fletcher, and Robert Herrick. In music we have William Byrd, Luca Marenzio, Cristo'bal Morales, John Shepherd, Giovanni Gabrieli, John Merbeck, Thomas Tallis, Thomas Morley, Thomas Weekes and Richard Farrant – composers whose music is still used regularly in our cathedrals and churches. Reproductions of the work of Hans Holbein and Nicholas Hilliard, and the use of Aubrey's *Brief Lives* for background material linked with displays of material from relevant *Jackdaws* will help give depth and purpose to even the most formalised study.

Thus one will find that when children are really engrossed in a theme their study will often go to quite surprising depths which in turn lead to unexpected discoveries about the period under review. The teacher's task, if this happens, is to advise on related topics which would be worthy of study. Story telling, though still important, is relegated to a secondary role. History is stories, but it is also something more.

As the group becomes involved in a particular period of the past, the interest of the children will diverge – John may be interested in houses, Mary in costume, Jack in furniture, Paul in street scenes and methods of travel and Jean in hairstyles. Other children may take poetry or music as the starting point for their work or the lives of scientists, explorers or religious leaders.

If the children are engaged in individual topics of the type listed above and illustrated here, much written work will result. Group study books are the most satisfactory way of presenting this. It is wise to collect the material over several weeks rather than mount the pieces haphazardly as and when they are produced. This means that 'chapters' can be devoted to particular topics with individual children being responsible for each section of the book.

The possibilities of work along these lines are, of course, limitless. Each historical epoch could be studied as well through its artists, craftsmen and poets as through its soldiers and politicians. Although I do not suggest that we should embrace the former group and ignore the latter, I do believe that environmental studies provide a good starting point for a deeper appreciation of all the arts. This will in turn give our children experience which will enable them to express themselves with greater sensitivity in words as well as paint. A creative environment is not just the odd drape of cloth surrounding an attractive pot, it is not just art materials readily available, it is not just the latest poetry book open on the library bookshelf – it is all that we bring to our teaching – words, sounds and sights.

Poetry

Descriptive

Anon	*An Old Soldier of the Queen's*
Walter de la Mare	*The Picture*
Henry Fielding	*Hunting Song*
R. Greene	*Sir Geoffrey Chaucer*
Keats	*Meg Merrilees*
Longfellow	*The Village Blacksmith*
J. B. Nichols	*On the Toilet Table of Queen Marie-Antoinette*
Andrew Young	*The Roman Wall*
	A Prehistoric Camp

Historical

Chaucer	*The Canterbury Tales* (extracts)
Cowper	*Boadicea*
Michael Drayton	*Agincourt*
Robert Graves	*1805*
Longfellow	*King Robert of Sicily*
Lydgate	*Harry before Agincourt*
Shakespeare	'Henry V before Harfleur' (*Henry V*, Act III, scene 1)
Charles Wolfe	*The Burial of Sir John Moore at Corunna*

Humorous

Anon	*Three Jovial Welshmen*
Robert Browning	*Muckle Mouth Meg*
A. A. Milne	*The Knight whose Armour didn't Squeak*
Siegfried Sassoon	*Noah*

Poetry

Lyrical

Blake	*Jerusalem*
G. K. Chesterton	*The Rolling English Road*
Padraic Colum	*Old Woman of the Roads*
Thomas Hardy	*Friends Beyond*
John Skelton	*To Mistress Margaret Hussey*

Mystery

Anon	*Tom O' Bedlam*
Charles Lamb	*Old Familiar Faces*
John Masefield	*The Dead Knight*
E. Robinson	*Two Men*
Wordsworth	*An Old Man*

Narrative

Anon	*Brennan on the Moor*
W. H. Auden	*The Quarry*
Blake	*The Chimney Sweeper*
Charles Causley	*Song of Samuel Sweet*
Alfred Noyes	*The Highwayman*
Edgar Allan Poe	*Annabel Lee*

Sir A. Conan Doyle	*The White Company*
Elizabeth I	Speech at Tilbury before the Armada
W. Fitzstephen	*Life and death of Thomas Becket*
Henry Fielding	*Joseph Andrews* (Chapter XII – on stage coaching)
Froissart	*Chronicles*
R. L. Green	*King Arthur*
Thomas Hardy	*Under the Greenwood Tree* (Chapter 2, Part 2 – on making shoes)
Rudyard Kipling	*Puck of Pook's Hill*
	Rewards and Fairies
Magnus Magnusson	*King Harald's Saga*
J. Prebble	*Culloden* (extracts from Chapter 2 – 'Drummossie Moor')
Dorothy Sayers	*The Song of Roland*
Sir Walter Scott	*Ivanhoe* (Chapter XIII – Robin Hood)
Tobias Smollett	*Roderick Random* (Chapter XXIV – on the press gang)
B. Stone (editor)	*Sir Gawain and the Green Knight*
T. H. White	*The Sword in the Stone*

KNIGHTS

Knights

I attempted in the opening section of this book to show how an interest in the past can lead to considerable historical research, to writing, model making and display, to listening to poetry and music and to making visits to places of interest in the school's immediate locality.

Yet one must not become so academic that the children's sense of magic is lost. One would, for example, present the highwayman as a cruel killer fit only for a dreadful death upon the gallows using scraps of the Newgate calendar or the *Gallows Tree* ballad for emphasis. But surely some romance should remain – such as the gripping ride to York by Dick Turpin or the lilting tunes from Gay's *The Beggar's Opera*. I need point the contrast no further – except to add that we should have a little of both when presenting these broad historical 'types' to children.

Let me be specific and suggest in detail how we could treat a theme which was based upon a historical occupation – knights and knight-hood. Where better to start than in the realms of magic with King Arthur, the Round Table and the Holy Grail. Here we have stories of wizards, dragons, princesses in danger, good knights and evil knights. Our literary heritage is rich in such stories and ballads, and there is little need to list them all here. I feel, however, that I should mention the following which perhaps are not used as widely as they might be. J. R. Tolkien's *The Lord of the Rings* is full of magic set in a land of make-believe and peopled by characters with strange sounding names – Wizard Gandalf, The Lords of Nazgul, Grond, the ram, 'fashioned in the dark smithies of Mordor'. From classical literature we can use extracts from *Sir Gawain and the Green Knight*, *King Harald's Saga*, *The Story of Beowulf*, and *The Song of Roland* (all published in the Penguin classics). Conan Doyle's *Sir Nigel* and *The White Company* are also rich sources of material while Kingley's *Hereward the Wake* presents a dramatic picture of the life of a soldier during the latter part of the eleventh century. The romantic story of Richard I and Blondel, the life of the jester Rahere who founded St Bartholomew's hospital in London, and the light-hearted adventures of Don Quixote are useful supplements to the examples given above.

The place that poetry can play in the study must not be ignored for it too contains much that is rich in stories of chivalry. This could range from Chaucer's *Knight's Prologue* and Spencer's *Faerie Queen* to *Eldorado* by Edgar Allen Poe and *The Knight Whose Armour Didn't Squeak* by A. A. Milne.

Music can be used to give depth and meaning to the total experience; William Walton's music to Henry V with its evocative sound pictures of preparations for battle, the charge of the French knights and the ensuing rout is probably the most useful record available for this particular theme.

On a gentler note there is the moving ballad of *The Three Ravens* (Peter, Paul and Mary).

All of this will need to be set in some historical framework. Consideration could be given to the sites of castles (relating this particularly to the school's immediate neighbourhood), the development of castle building, methods of siege and defence, life inside a castle (*Katherine* by Anya Seton provides background here) supplemented by displays of pictures and relevant source books. I have found *Pictorial Education* with its attractive double page reproductions particularly valuable in this connection. Film strips will also add greatly to the childrens' appreciation of the period. Some have been made from stills from commercial films – Thomas à Becket's quarrel with Henry II is portrayed particularly brilliantly (Educational Productions Ltd, Wakefield, Yorks). Other topics which might develop from the study include arms and armour, heraldry, the crusades, the orders of knighthood, the duties of a page . . . the list is almost limitless for it could embrace the whole of English history from the time of Guthrum to the Great Civil War.

How can we use this for work in arts and crafts? In painting we could concentrate on the representation of historical scenes – but this to my mind is rather sterile, as it will push the children towards the copying of line drawings from history books. I have found that large-scale figures from metallic paper gives much greater scope. These could simply be mounted on a sheet of sugar paper or glued onto cardboard cut out so that they are largely free standing. Bottle tops, smoothed flat, make excellent chain mail and can be glued on almost any grease-free surface with Rowney's 'PVA medium' or Margro's 'Marvin'. Castles – particularly the central keep – constructed from large packing cases are another popular activity. A light cover of paste and paper scraps will give an excellent painting surface (and if a mixture of detergent and powder colour is used for painting a realistic stone finish will be achieved).

Wire figures (18 gauge, obtainable from most ironmongers by the 1 lb coil) could also be made. Only the hands and feet need be fashioned – the rest of the frame being dressed with fabric scraps or coloured paper (see plate). Another approach could be through brass rubbings. This will obviously depend greatly upon the locality of the school. Some areas (North Essex, Suffolk) are rich in knightly brasses, others are quite devoid of them. Always get permission before allowing children to take rubbings. Detail paper (obtainable from most artist colourmen) should be used. I prefer to let children rub with black crayon (Finart range) than with heelball which is rather hard and therefore more difficult for young children to handle. (Heelball is made from beeswax, tallow and lamp black by Philips and Page Ltd., 50, Kensington Church Street, London W.8 for the Monumental Brass Society.)

Writing can, of course, flow from all these activities. It might take the form of direct description recorded on tape of an episode in the life of a knight – a tourney, a siege, a meal in the great hall. It could be an account of an adventure with a fantastic creature, it might retell Beowulf's struggle with Grendel. But whatever is written will be enriched by the childrens' direct involvement in some of the activities described above.

Music

Composer	Title of work
Bruckner	Scherzo from *Symphony No. 4, The Romantic*
Hanson	*Lament for Beowulf*
Richard Strauss	*Don Quixote*
Wagner	*Lohengrin*, extracts
Walton	Incidental music to *Henry V* and *Hamlet*

Poetry and Prose – See *People Long Ago*.

Toys and Toyshops

Toys and Toyshops

Much of the work I have described so far has been more appropriate to the older children in the Primary Department. I therefore now propose to redress the balance and consider some activities suitable for 8-and 9-year olds.

Some time ago Margaret Hutchings wrote a book entitled *The Book of the Teddy Bear* (Mills and Boon). It is a collection of patterns for making bears of all shapes and sizes from complicated jointed bears to simple bears made from two pieces of material (which seven-and eight-year-olds could manage without difficulty). What intrigued me, however, were the statistics which were included in the text. For example, I learned that only 10 per cent of Primary School children in a sample poll did not have a Teddy Bear, 5 per cent had more than one – and one child possessed eight. Among well-known personalities who still possess bears are Lady Butler (who owns Buffs) and John Betjeman (Archibald Ormsby Gore) while Mr Woppitt (the fastest bear on earth) spent part of his life in the cockpit of Donald Campbell's *Bluebird*. This led me to examine the possibility of using a toy theme for creative work and it is surprising how many avenues there are to follow and it is well to remember that soft toy making need not be restricted to teddy bears and dolls, more exotic animals are equally easy to make. There are a whole range of source books for the teacher to use. The list below is by no means exhaustive but it does indicate possible lines of approach.

Anne Butler: *Teaching Children Embroidery* (Studio Vista)
Winsome Douglas: *Toys For Your Delight*
Margaret Hutchings: *Dolls And How To Make Them* (Mills and Boon)
Barbara Snook: *Creative Soft Toys* (Batsford)
Six Woolly Dolls (Dryad); *Rag Bag Dolls* (Dryad); *Circus Toys* (Dryad)

Materials for this work do not present a problem – scissors and needles, embroidery cottons in a variety of colours, sequins for decoration, felt scraps and soft flock. (Foam or old stockings are an adequate substitute although it is difficult to stuff hard with these materials.) If each child keeps her work in a large envelope storage is easy and the fact that it can be taken out as a fill-in activity for wet lunch times makes me really enthusiastic about it!

Toy making in other materials is also popular – the junk lesson can be used as a starting point for work in wood (provided, of course, suitable tools are available). Winifred Horton's *Wooden Toy Making* (Dryad) will be particularly useful for teachers who have little experience in wood-working techniques. It is also worth remembering that now that acrylic paints are generally available, glueing and painting wooden toys presents no difficulty.

There are a number of musical links with this theme. Rossini-Respighi's ballet *La Boutique Fantasque* is set in a toy shop. *Coppelia* (music by Delibes) relies upon an equally strange story. Coppelius the toymaker is making life-like dolls. His secret is discovered by Franz, a lad who falls in love with a beautiful girl in Coppelius' window. He discovers that the object of his passion is nothing more than a clockwork doll. Another ballet in which toys come to life is *The Nutcracker* (Tchaikovsky). The battle between the toys and the mice is probably the best scene for mime, picture-making and writing but the suite contains an overture and the dances Sugar Plum, Russian, Arab, Chinese and Reed pipes, which might also inspire work with brighter children.

Children often 'talk' to their toys in play, like John Betjeman who describes how Archibald's 'half moon ears received my confidence' (*Summoned by Bells*, published by John Murray). Free writing based on the character of the children's own toys and the adventures they have together will probably lead the more gifted members of the class to write their own versions of *The Nutcracker*, *Coppelia* and *La Boutique Fantasque*.

Music

Composer	Title of work
Bizet	*Children's Games* (piano duet version)
	No. 2. 'Jimbo'
	No. 3. 'Serenade for the Doll'
	No. 6. 'Golliwogs Cake Walk'
Delibes	*Coppélia*
Elgar	'Hobby Horse' from *The Nursery Suite*
Fauré	*Dolly Suite*
Gounod	*Funeral March of a Marionette*
Haydn	*Toy Symphony*
Rossini–Respighi	*La Boutique Fantasque*
Schumann	*Scenes of Childhood*, No. 9. 'Knight of the Hobby Horse'
Tchaikovsky	*The Nutcracker Suite*

Poetry

Descriptive

E. Jennings	*Kites*
A. A. Milne	*Fly my Kite*
James Reeves	*Fireworks*
E. V. Rieu	*The Paint Box*
Robert Louis Stevenson	*The Swing*
Oscar Wilde	*Balloons*

Lyrical

Anon	*I Had a Little Nut Tree*
E. E. Cummings	*In Just Spring*
Robert Herrick	*Stool Ball*
Charles Kingsley	*I Once Had a Beautiful Doll Dear*
Edith Sitwell	*The King of China's Daughter*

Narrative

Robert Graves	*Penny Fiddle*

Author's Note: There is a quantity of verse of indifferent quality which could also be used to illustrate this theme. These I have deliberately omitted.

Prose

M. Bond	*Paddington* Stories
C. Collodi	*Pinocchio*
D. H. Lawrence	*The Rockinghorse Winner*
A. A. Milne	*Winnie the Pooh*

Appendix 1

CHILDREN'S WRITING

It is almost impossible to evaluate children's writing without an intimate knowledge of the children who produce it. The examples here were written by London children and are included to indicate the type of writing which often flows from the thematic approach I have outlined in the previous pages.

The original layout of the writing (lines, stanzas, etc.,) has been preserved – although the spelling has been rationalised in one or two instances. Although purists may jibe at this I believe that words are meant to communicate feelings – and a written South London accent (the mind boggles!) would be impossible for many of my readers to follow.

Nineteen Floors Up   Deborah (Aged 9)

Black, blue, white and brown
Are the rooves of London town
I can see where the old folk live
High buildings
Low buildings
Smoke from chimneys mix with clouds
I felt sick when I looked down
Nineteen floors up.

Shopping Day   Stephen (Aged 9)

Combing her hair stood Miss Johnson ready to go shopping
Turning off the gas
Picking up her purse
Putting on her coat
She walked out the door with her bag
Remembering she had to get a new hat. She walked in
'She asked if they had a hat to fit her
The shop assistant said 'yes'
She brought an enormous box
Full of hats
She fiddled about with them trying them on . . .
Then to the Chemists
'A bottle of Penicillin please'

'How much'
'Seven shillings'. She gave him the money and walked to the Butchers
There stood the fat jolly butcher
There was always a smile on his face
'A leg of Mutton please'
'6/6d' he said and wrapped it up. She put it by the loaf, the hat
the Penicillin. Home. She opened the door
Walked in
Put on the kettle
Took off her shoes
And put down her basket
And had a nice cup of tea.

Wet Streets
Jennifer (Aged 10)

I stepped off the bus and the bitter wind tore at my clothing. As I walked my shoes clattered on the wet pavement. The wind was strong, forcing me to bow my head to protect my hair. I felt damp, cold and uncomfortable because my wet clothes clung to me. The smell of rain, hair and damp gaberdine . . . . At last I was home. I knocked at the door. My Mother opened it. I looked at the warm fire and was comforted.

The Sea
Barry (Aged 7)

The wind shakes the sea
And all ships rock over
He crashes and splashes at the lonely rocks
Sea gulls scream out
Great waves splash over the ships
Great black skies come up

The Sea
Susan (Aged 8)

The sea is like a ragged dog biting the stones.
It rolls over the sands washing them up and down.
It tries to escape but rolls back to his hole.
Always trying, but never capturing the shore.
Then it gives up
And calms down.

Shell

Robert (Aged 9)

Spiky shell
Like a spiky ball
Smooth and delicate walls inside
Like a pot which has just been varnished
Ugly on one side
And rough
But beautiful on the other.

Just lying at my feet.

Shadow Land

Lisa (Aged 9)

On Monday morning
getting up from bed
I saw my shadow on
the wall. I saw a crack
it began to get bigger.
A door appeared in front
of me. It was the shape
of my shadow. It opened.
I looked in it, then I
stepped inside. It was
a long passage. I was
frightened in there. I
saw hundreds of shadows, there
were dogs shadows, cats, cows all sorts of
shadows. Then I saw my own. I did not know where I was
until I saw a little man who told me I was in Shadow Land.
It is a long way from London he said.

A Fear

Diana (Aged 9)

I could hardly believe my eyes when I found myself at the bottom of a well.
The strange thing about it was that there was no water in it. About 3 ft
above me was a door. The whole well was about 100 ft deep, but when I
saw this door I climbed up and tried to open it. It opened quite easily.
I looked inside. It was quite light so I walked in and then the door closed.
I tried to open it but I was locked in. I saw something coming towards me,
it started to walk more quickly, and then . . .

Time Machine

Martin (Aged 9)

Suddenly I realised that they had moved it. They had stolen it from me. As I ran I was trembling with fright. I kept on running. I knew it was stolen. I felt it in my blood. I ran until I couldn't breathe, until I was gasping for breath. Then I got to the spot where I left my Time Machine. It was gone!! I saw something, a glittering statue in ice. It started to melt. It was my Time Machine. I got in it and went back to my own time.

The Attack

Kevin (Aged 10)

There were thousands and thousands of men dressed in black. Every one of them hooded. They crashed at the walls again and again. But they could not break the metal doors of our city. We were more skilled than they were and we had caterpults and long bows. Gradually they advanced, but still they could not break the doors. But there was one of them who had the blackest horse and the blackest coat and the blackest hood. All the others had heads but he did not, he also had a large crown on his hood instead of a head. He had a large ball of fire and his sword was covered in flames.

The Thing

Andrew (Aged 11)

It was green, pink, all colours but somehow no colour. It was what I had thought it would look like. It was the 0603635. It had six arms, and eight legs. Its face (if that was what you could call it) was upside down. Its mouth was like Raspberry ripple Rolle. It was on a machine that was hard to describe. Imagine a gramophone record on wheels, with a rolled up newspaper on the front. Beside 0603635 was a box with dials and levers and switches of all shapes and sizes. It moved towards me. I started to run. It was gaining on me. It got hold of me and . . .

David and Goliath

Dorothy (Aged 7)

The giant that David was to kill
Was a big strong man
He held out his hand
And said 'I rule the land'
There he stood upon the hill
David there was to kill
'You do not rule the land' he said
'And now you will be stone dead'
So there he threw a stone at his head
And there he lay with a stone at his head

The giant was dead
That David had to kill
Up on the hill

At Home in 1640

Ralph (Aged 9)

I watched the wood fire crackle and flicker and the candle melt away.
The wind was howling and beating against the shutters. I walked to the
fire place where the flames leapt up the big chimney. I poured out the ale.
I drank it, listening to Father talking about Cromwell. 'Up to bed now'
said Mother. I kissed my parents good night and climbed the big staircase
to my room. Before huddling beneath the covers I peered out of the window.
The soldier was still on guard!

A Strange Fruit

Francesca (Aged 9)

On our table was a strange fruit. It was a sort of yellowy brown. It felt hard
and smelt like a lemon and had some little roots coming out of the top. We
cut it. We were all waiting to see what was in it. It fell in half. Inside was
juice like blood and a pattern like a flower, with all little pips in it. It just
tasted like water. We smelt it again. It smelt like earth and musty. It was
lovely to taste though.

The Frog

Virginia (Aged 7)

Slimy, slithery, sloppy, shimmery
is the frog
Wet wobbly jumpy probably
Big eyed
Whether you like him
Or whether you not
So much to say –
Oh such a lot
The frog –
Creeping around in such a way
It seems to make you say Hooray!
Shiny greenish yellowish
He creeps around
His smiling face from eye to eye
From ear to ear

Breathing easily
Yes breathing heavily
The frog!

Hoppity, Hoppity, Hop

Lindsey (Aged 7)

In Spring I went to the country
And there I saw a rabbit
   Hoppity, Hoppity, Hop
I saw his little white tail bobbing
As he went
   Hoppity, hoppity, Hop
He crept out of his burrow
And heard a noise
   Hoppity, Hoppity, Hop
He stamped, he winked
Down his hole he dashed
   Hoppity, Hoppity, Hop.

Hunted

Catherine (Aged 10)

I turned to my den, but that was blocked.
I kept on running, I could not stop.
I passed many chickens as I went by
But I could not stop or I would die.
Up hill and down
Would I now fail
I turned again but –
Their feet were like thunder
Death, death, death
Rang the throb of my heart
I and my family would soon for ever part

The Wind

Simon (Aged 7)

O wind I saw you toss them high
I saw the kites in the sky
O wind you are cold
Are you young or old?
I hear you blow past
In the grass,
Up on the hill

124

You blow the wind-mill
It histles,
It whistles,
And every one said
I wish that wind was in his bed
He tossed the boats on the sea
And said 'what a fellow' said he.

Spell   Robert (Aged 9)

Take
> The vein of a cat
> Rats eyes
> Dogs ears
> Hearts of snakes
> Pigs livers
> Bones of ants
> Claw of bat
> Spiders legs
> Creeping bugs

Grind, mix and grind again
Add water to the brew
Heat over an open fire
Use while warm on bites and breaks, bones and sores.

Strange Lady   Jacqueline (Aged 9)

'You know the girl I'm talking of – Jannet Jourdmayne. She lives in an old
barn across the field all by herself. Some people say she makes stew out of
animal bones. She's a pretty girl really but she does not care how she looks.
They say she keeps beetles in her shoes and prays to the sun. Quick. Hide.
Here she comes.'

Transformation   Jayne (Aged 10)

The spell began to work
I felt not at all like myself
I could see my hands were changing
They were changing into something
It was something like cats hands
I had done it

I was a cat now
But the spell did not work for long
Then just as suddenly I was back to my old self again.

Psalm

Anne (Aged 11)

Let me be at the place of the cottage
Let it rise from a garden
Let the garden have flowers
Let the flowers be red, orange, violet
Let there be a little gate at the end of the garden
Let the gate lead to a road
Let the road lead to shops
Let the shops have another road leading to a market
Let the market have stalls
Let the stalls have toys, food, groceries, clothes
Let there be a road with grass along the side where the horses and cows can go
Let there be little ducks wandering along the road
Let me be in the cottage with a baby
Let the cottage be where I can find it
Where it can be within me
Let me be where it is

The Door

Go and open the door
Maybe you'll see some birds flying
In a misty blue sky
Go and open the door
Maybe you'll see feet running madly
Over the dusty floor
Go and open the door
Maybe you'll hear voices
Coming from all directions
Go and open the door
Maybe you'll see a horse
Romping over a mat of green grass
Go and open the door
I'm sure you'll see something
Go and open the door

Carol (Aged 11)

Appendix 2

MUSIC

This list of music is not meant to be exhaustive but it will provide the basis for considerable creative experience along the lines suggested in this book – as well as meeting the needs of assembly times and incidental music for class and school drama productions.

Many of the recordings will be available through local libraries. The sleeves often provide background information sufficient to meet the needs of both teacher and child. Most of the pieces are also to be found listed under the themes considered in this book.

Composer	Title of work
Isaac Albéniz	*Iberia*
Malcolm Arnold	*Tam O'Shanter*
J. S. Bach	Music from *St John Passion*
	St Matthew Passion
Balakirev	*Islamey*
Bartók	*Dance Suite*
Bax	*Tintagel*
Beethoven	Extracts from *Symphony No. 6*
	Egmont Overture
	Piano sonata in C Sharp Minor (Moonlight)
Berlioz	'Royal Hunt and Storm' from *The Trojans*
	Roman Carnival
	L'Enfance du Christ (extracts)
	Symphonie Fantastique
Bizet	*L'Arlésienne*
	Jeux d'Enfants suite
Bliss	*Colour Symphony*
Borodin	*In the Steppes of Central Asia*
	Polovtsian Dances
Britten	*Noye's Fludde*
	Four Sea Interludes
	The Prince of the Pagodas

Composer	Title of work
Coates	*Three Elizabeths Suite*
	Three Bears Suite
Coleridge-Taylor	*Hiawatha's Wedding Feast*
Copland	*Rodeo*
Debussy	*La Mer*
	Images No. 1, Set 1
	Images No. 3, Set 2
	Prelude à l'après-midi d'un Faune
	Children's Corner Suite
	Extracts from *Pelléas et Mélisande*
Delius	*Hassan*
	Brigg Fair
Dukas	*L'Apprenti Sorcier*
Dvořák	*Slavonic Dances*
Elgar	*Wand of Youth* Suite
	Extracts from *Enigma Variations*
Falla	*The Three-Cornered Hat*
Gershwin	*Rhapsody in Blue*
Grainger	*Shepherd's Hay*
Grétry	Extracts from *Zémire et Azor*
Grieg	*Peer Gynt*
Handel	*Royal Fireworks*
	Water Music
	The Arrival of the Queen of Sheba
Haydn	*Toy Symphony*
	The Creation (excerpts)
Holst	*The Planets Suite*
Honegger	*Pacific 231*
Humperdinck	*Hansel & Gretel*
Khatchaturian	Dances from ballet *Gayaneh* e.g. 'Sabre Dance'
Kodály	*Háry János* Suite
Mendelssohn	*A Midsummer Night's Dream*
	The Hebrides ('Fingal's Cave')
Mozart	Overtures to:
	Die Entführung aus dem Serail
	Figaro
	Don Giovanni
	Così fan tutte
	The Magic Flute

Composer	Title of work
Mussorgsky	Extracts from *Boris Godounov*
	Pictures at an Exhibition
	Night on the Bare Mountain
Offenbach	Extracts from *La Grande Duchess de*
	Gérolstein
	Orpheus in the Underworld
Prokofiev	*The Love of Three Oranges*
	Lieutenant Kije
	Peter and the Wolf
Quilter	*Children's Overture*
Ravel	*Bolero*
	Mother Goose Suite
	Pavane pour une enfante défunte
	L'Enfant et les Sortilèges
Rimsky-Korsakov	*The Golden Cockerel*
	Scheherazade
Rossini	*William Tell* (storm)
Saint-Saëns	*Carnival of Animals*
	Danse Macabre
Schumann	*Kinderscenen*
Sibelius	*Valse Triste*
	Karelia Suite
	The Swan of Tuonela
Smetana	'Vltava' from *Má Vlast*
Stravinsky	*The Fire Bird*
	Petrouchka
	The Rite of Spring
	The Soldier's Tale
Tchaikovsky	'*1812*' *Overture*
	Casse Noisette
	Swan Lake
Vaughan Williams	*The Wasps* Overture
	Symphony No. 7, Antarctica
Wagner	*The Flying Dutchman* (extracts)
Walton	*Façade* (Suite)
	Façade with Edith Sitwell
	Incidental music to *Henry V*
	Hamlet
	Belshazzar's Feast
Weinberger	*Schwanda the Bagpiper*

Appendix 3

BIBLIOGRAPHY

Author	Title	Publisher
Adland, D.	*Group Drama*	Longmans
Alexander, E. & Carter, B.	*Art for Young People*	Mills and Boon
Ash, B. & Rapaport, B.	*Creative Work in the Junior School*	Methuen
Dean, J.	*Art & Craft in the Primary School*	A. & C. Black
Gibbs, E.	*Teaching of Art in School*	William and Norgate
Gray, V. & Percival, R.	*Music, Movement and Mime*	Oxford
Jorden, D.	*Childhood and Movement*	Blackwell
Hartman, G. & Schumaker, A.	*Creative Expression in the Development of Children*	Hall & Co.
Marshall, S.	*Experiment in Education*	C.U.P.
	Aspects of Art Work	Evans
Melzi, K.	*Art in the Primary School*	Blackwell
Morris, D.	*Biology of Art*	Methuen
Petrie, M.	*Art and Regeneration*	Paul Elek
	Child Art to Man Art	Paul Elek
Pluckrose, H.	*Creative Art & Craft*	Macdonald
	Let's Make Pictures	Mills & Boon
	Let's Work Large	Mills & Boon
Read, H.	*Education through Art*	Faber
Richardson, M.	*Art and the Child*	U.L.P.
Sealey, L.	*Creative Use of Mathematics*	Blackwell
Steveni, M.	*Art and Education*	Batsford
Tomlinson, R.	*Picture & Pattern Making*	U.L.P.
Tomlinson, R. & Mills, J.	*Growth of Child Art*	U.L.P.
Yglesias, J.	*Education for Living*	Cory Adams

Also

The 'Introducing' series, published by B. T. Batsford (London) and Watson-Gupthill (New York). This series covers a whole range of basic art techniques.

Children and their Primary Schools   HMSO 1966.
Primary Education   a handbook of suggestions for teachers   HMSO 1959.